IFIP Advances in Information and Communication Technology   **760**

Editor-in-Chief

Kai Rannenberg, Goethe University Frankfurt, Germany

IFIP Advances in Information and Communication Technology

The IFIP AICT series publishes state-of-the-art results in the sciences and technologies of information and communication. The scope of the series includes: foundations of computer science; software theory and practice; education; computer applications in technology; communication systems; systems modeling and optimization; information systems; ICT and society; computer systems technology; security and protection in information processing systems; artificial intelligence; and human-computer interaction.

Edited volumes and proceedings of refereed international conferences in computer science and interdisciplinary fields are featured. These results often precede journal publication and represent the most current research.

The principal aim of the IFIP AICT series is to encourage education and the dissemination and exchange of information about all aspects of computing.

More information about this series at https://link.springer.com/bookseries/6102

Marco A. Wehrmeister · Stefan Henkler ·
Márcio Kreutz · Marcelo Götz · Achim Rettberg
Editors

Architecting the Future: Intelligent Systems for Embedded AI, Autonomous Technologies, and Digital Twins

8th IFIP TC 10 International
Embedded Systems Symposium, IESS 2024
Gainesville, FL, USA, October 14–15, 2024
Proceedings

Springer

Editors
Marco A. Wehrmeister ⓘ
Federal University of Technology – Parana
Curitiba, Paraná, Brazil

Márcio Kreutz ⓘ
Federal University of Rio Grande do Norte
Natal, Rio Grande do Norte, Brazil

Achim Rettberg
Hamm-Lippstadt University of Applied
Sciences
Hamm, Germany

Stefan Henkler
Hamm-Lippstadt University of Applied
Sciences
Hamm, Germany

Marcelo Götz ⓘ
Federal University of Rio Grande do Sul
Porto Alegre, Rio Grande do Sul, Brazil

ISSN 1868-4238   ISSN 1868-422X (electronic)
IFIP Advances in Information and Communication Technology
ISBN 978-3-032-07101-9   ISBN 978-3-032-07102-6 (eBook)
https://doi.org/10.1007/978-3-032-07102-6

This Springer imprint is published by the registered company Springer Nature Switzerland AG
The registered company address is: Gewerbestrasse 11, 6330 Cham, Switzerland

If disposing of this product, please recycle the paper.

Preface

This book compiles the research and technical works presented at the International Embedded Systems Symposium (IESS) 2024. The event enabled deep and fruitful discussions on innovative aspects of modern embedded and cyber-physical systems. The chapters highlight tendencies and solutions for industry-relevant problems, ranging from hardware acceleration for image processing to simulated environments using Digital Twins and UAV systems. All these aspects were discussed under the emerging influences of Artificial Intelligence and Cybersecurity.

A broad discussion on the design, analysis, and verification of embedded and cyber-physical systems is presented in a complementary view throughout the chapters of this book. The presented research and technical works cover system-level design methods, algorithms, verification and validation techniques, estimation of system properties and characteristics, performance analysis, and real-time systems design. Also, the book presents industrial and real-world application case studies that discuss the challenges and realizations of modern embedded systems, especially when it comes to including artificial intelligence algorithms and techniques in embedded systems.

The technological advances over recent years have provided a resourceful infrastructure to embedded systems in terms of an enormous amount of processing and storage capacity. Formerly external components are now integrated into a single System-on-Chip that includes various hardware accelerators such as video decoders, and artificial intelligence co-processors. This tendency results in a dramatic reduction in the size and cost of embedded systems. Such a hardware infrastructure enables an increasing number of provided services, allowing embedded systems to enter a lot of application areas (including cyber-physical applications). As a unique technology, the design of embedded systems is an essential element of many innovations.

Embedded systems meet their performance goals, including real-time constraints, employing a combination of special-purpose hardware and software components tailored to the system requirements. Both the development of new features and the reuse of existing intellectual property components are essential to keeping up with ever-demanding customer requirements. Furthermore, design complexities are steadily growing with an increasing number of components that must cooperate properly. Novel integrated co-design approaches are deemed necessary to further improve the design flow while reducing the project's overall cost.

Embedded system designers must cope with multiple goals and constraints simultaneously, including timing, power, reliability, dependability, maintenance, packaging, and, last but not least, price. Safety, security, and privacy are mandatory requirements for modern applications, which also demand different levels of intelligence and autonomy. The significance and importance of these constraints vary depending on the target application area. Typical embedded applications include consumer electronics, automotive, avionics, medical, industrial automation, robotics, communication devices, autonomous transportation systems, and others.

The International Embedded Systems Symposium (IESS) is a unique forum to present novel ideas, exchange timely research results, and discuss the state of the art and future trends in the field of embedded systems. Contributors and participants from both industry and academia take an active part in this symposium. The IESS conference is organized by the Computer Systems Technology committee (TC10) of the International Federation for Information Processing (IFIP), especially the Working Group 10.2 "Embedded Systems".

IESS is a truly interdisciplinary conference on the design of embedded systems. Computer Science and Electrical Engineering are the predominant academic disciplines concerned with the topics covered in IESS, but many applications also involve civil, mechanical, aerospace, and automotive engineering, as well as various medical disciplines.

In 2005, IESS was held for the first time in Manaus, Brazil. In this initial installment, IESS 2005 was very successful with 30 accepted papers ranging from specification to embedded systems applications. IESS 2007 was the second edition of the symposium held in Irvine (CA), the USA with 35 accepted papers and 2 tutorials ranging from analysis and design methodologies to case studies from automotive and medical applications. IESS 2009 took place in the wonderful Schoß Montfort in Langenargen, Germany with 28 accepted papers and 2 tutorials ranging from efficient modeling towards challenges for designers of fault-tolerant embedded systems. IESS 2013 was held in Paderborn, Germany, at the Heinz Nixdorf Museums-Forum (HNF) with 22 full papers, and 8 short papers. IESS 2015 was held in Foz do Iguaçu, Brazil, close to the beautiful Iguaçu Falls, with 12 full papers and 6 short papers. In 2019, IESS was held in Friedrichshafen, Germany, with 16 full papers and 4 short papers selected and presented at the symposium. The 7th edition, IESS 2022, was held at the University of Hamm-Lippstadt, Germany, with 10 full papers and two short papers.

The eighth edition of IESS, held in 2024 at the University of Florida, USA, featured a rigorous review process overseen by the technical program committee. Each paper underwent comprehensive double-blind evaluation by three to four experts in the relevant subject areas. As a result, nine full papers were selected for inclusion from ten submissions. Additionally, two keynote presentations on AI and Cybersecurity underscored the high quality of the conference.

The technical program of IESS 2024 has included sessions about Digital Twins and UAVs applied to simulated and urban systems, innovative architectures for Deep Learning Efficiency and Architectures and Integration of Intelligent Embedded Systems. Last but not least, the scientific and technical papers were presented and stimulated a deep and insightful discussion between the presenters and the attendees.

All authors of this book volume cited below, besides their formal roles in the organization of IESS 2024, were involved in the discussions and decisions made about the analysis of review results, the organization of this book's chapters, and the writing of this preface. Since we are a small group that is involved in the organization of this conference, this has been usual in all previous, as well as for the current IESS edition.

In summary, excited about our strong technical program, we had a highly successful IESS 2024 conference with fruitful and lively discussions.

May 2025

Marco A. Wehrmeister
Stefan Henkler
Márcio Kreutz
Marcelo Götz
Achim Rettberg

Organization

General Chairs

Marco A. Wehrmeister   Federal University of Technology - Paraná, Brazil
Stefan Henkler   Hamm-Lippstadt University of Applied Sciences, Germany

Program Chairs

Marcio Kreutz   Federal University of Rio Grande do Norte, Brazil
Tim Shattkowsky   Hamm-Lippstadt University of Applied Sciences, Germany

Technical Program Committee

Michael Amann	ZF Friedrichshafen, Germany
Jürgen Becker	Karlsruhe Institute of Technology, Germany
Christophe Bobda	University of Florida, USA
Luigi Carro	Federal University of Rio Grande do Sul, Brazil
Florian Dittmann	STABIL GROUP International GmbH, Germany
Rainer Doemer	University of California at Irvine, USA
Michel Dos Santos Soares	Federal University of Sergipe, Brazil
Edison P. de Freitas	Federal University of Rio Grande do Sul, Brazil
Masahiro Fujita	University of Tokyo, Japan
Marcelo Götz	Federal University of Rio Grande do Sul, Brazil
Andreas Gerstlauer	University of Texas Austin, USA
Kim Grüttner	OFFIS, Germany
Stefan Henkler	Hamm-Lippstadt University of Applied Sciences, Germany
Paula Herber	University of Münster, Germany
Carsten Homburg	dSPACE, Germany
Uwe Honekamp	Vector Informatik, Germany
Michael Huebner	Ruhr University Bochum, Germany
Marcio Kreutz	Federal University of Rio Grande do Norte, Brazil
Thomas Lehmann	HAW Hamburg, Germany
Jose Lima	Polytechnic Institute of Bragança, Portugal

Contents

Architectures and Integration
for Intelligent Embedded Systems

Automated Integration of Safety Mechanisms into Functional Software for Safety-Relevant Systems

Rolf Schmedes[(✉)] [iD], Gregor Nitsche [iD], Ralf Stemmer [iD], and Kim Grüttner [iD]

German Aerospace Center, Cologne, Germany
{rolf.schmedes,gregor.nitsche,ralf.stemmer,kim.gruettner}@dlr.de

Abstract. In the development of safety-relevant systems, the integration of safety software into functional software is crucial for reliable and safe operation. This paper presents a novel semi-automated process designed to integrate software safety mechanisms into safety-relevant systems efficiently. Leveraging a model-driven engineering approach, the method initially separates functional and safety source code and then subsequently combines them in a semi-automated weaving step, producing functionally safe source code, ready for compilation. This approach incorporates expert safety engineering knowledge during the setup phase, facilitating the integration process. The proposed methodology not only enhances cost-effectiveness and reduces human error but also supports the quick evaluation of various safety configurations. A proof-of-concept implementation, demonstrated with an adaptive cruise control system, illustrates the practical application and effectiveness of this method. Future work will explore the preservation of timing behavior when retrofitting safety mechanisms, potentially extending the applicability of this approach to further use cases.

Keywords: Model-Driven Engineering · Code Generation · Safety Software · Embedded Systems

1 Introduction

Functionally safe software is designed and implemented to operate correctly and reliably, especially in critical or hazardous situations where failures could result in harm, injury, or damage. It aims to minimize the risk of failures and ensures that the software behaves predictably, even in the presence of faults or errors. Functionally safe software is the combination of functional software and safety software.

The development of functionally safe software is in general a complex endeavour. Functional requirements and safety requirements can be contradictory to each other and require a complex, holistic analysis. The same holds true on a software level. Modifications to the functional code can impact safety mechanisms and vice versa. Changes must be carefully analyzed to ensure they don't compromise safety requirements or introduce new risks. A systematic separation

© IFIP International Federation for Information Processing 2026
Published by Springer Nature Switzerland AG 2026
M. A. Wehrmeister et al. (Eds.): IESS 2024, IFIP AICT 760, pp. 3–14, 2026.
https://doi.org/10.1007/978-3-032-07102-6_1

between functional and safety software could mitigate the complexity, increase the maintainability and the likelihood of reuse.

In order to develop software for safety-relevant systems, it is essential to adhere to international standards, such as IEC 61508 [10] for general industrial applications, ISO 26262 [11] for automotive systems, or DO-178C [7] for avionics software. These standards dictate a strictly systematic development process and require the implementation of certain software safety mechanisms to minimize risk. This results in a fixed set of safety mechanisms used in developing safety-relevant systems aiming for certification. Depending on the required risk minimization, more or fewer mechanisms from this set are relevant. However, because safety software and functional software are closely integrated, reuse is uncommon, and safety mechanisms are manually reimplemented for each project. This presents an untapped potential for automation, which could lead to significant cost savings.

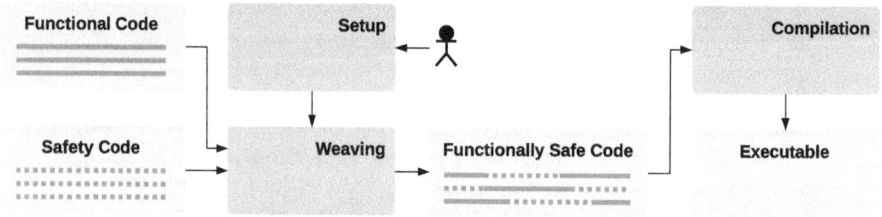

Fig. 1. Fundamental Idea of the Approach

In this paper we present a semi-automated process for integrating software safety mechanisms for safety-relevant systems. The basic idea is depicted in Fig. 1. Functional source code and safety source code are initially considered separately. Both aspects of the source code are then combined in a semi-automated weaving step, leading to a source-to-source transformation, which produces functionally safe source code that can then be compiled as usual. Expert knowledge of a safety engineer will be incorporated into the weaving step via a setup option. The proposed approach enables the efficient and therefore more cost-effective integration of safety software. In addition, the systematic and automated procedures allow for easy and quick evaluation of different safety configurations, while reducing the likelihood for human error and improving the overall quality of the code base. Moreover, the presented approach can be used for retrofitting software safety mechanisms to existing systems since it works on already existing source code.

The structure of this paper is as follows: First, the relevant context for the problem and the selected software safety mechanisms are described in Sect. 2. The approach section (Sect. 3) describes the process and the utilized models. A proof-of-concept implementation of the approach in C++ is then briefly summarized in Sect. 4 using the example of an adaptive cruise controller. The second to last Sect. 5 discusses related research work. Finally, the paper concludes by summarizing the results and offering suggestions for future research and improvements.

2 Background

The background chapter is divided into two sections. First, it describes how functionally safe software is usually developed. The second section presents an overview of software safety mechanisms required by common standards.

2.1 State-of-the-Art Safety Engineering

Numerous safety standards exist to reduce the likelihood of safety-relevant system failures. These standards offer guidelines for designing, implementing, and maintaining such systems. The subsequent sections will provide an overview of the IEC 61508 standard.

The fundamental principle of IEC 61508 requires that any safety-related system should either function correctly or fail predictably and safely under all possible stated conditions. The standard outlines a thorough engineering process known as the safety life cycle, consisting of 16 phases to achieve this objective. Beginning with analysis, progressing through principles for realization, and concluding with stages related to system operation.

An essential aspect of this life cycle is a hazard and risk analysis, involving a probabilistic failure approach to categorize the safety implications of a component's failure. It consists of three key stages: hazard identification, analysis, and risk assessment. For the risk assessment, risk is considered as a function of the likelihood of a hazardous event and the severity of its consequences. The assessment can be done either with qualitative or quantitative analysis techniques. This evaluation helps identify risks that need mitigation, enabling the design of appropriate safety software and thereby reduces the likelihood of under- or overuse of software safety mechanisms. The required risk reduction is then translated into a target safety integrity level (SIL). SILs are discrete levels (ranging from SIL 1 to SIL 4) that represent the relative levels of risk-reduction provided by a safety function. The underlying rationale for SILs is hereby as follows: to achieve a higher risk reduction, the safety-related system must have a higher reliability, which requires a correspondingly higher target SIL.

IEC 61508 and other relevant safety standards provide guidance on the selection of software safety mechanisms to achieve a specified SIL. As a result, there exists a recurrent set of software safety mechanisms frequently used in the development of safety-related systems. An overview of those software safety mechanisms is given in the next section.

2.2 Software Safety Mechanisms Commonly Used

To gather an understanding of the mechanisms that a semi-automated approach for integrating software safety mechanisms would have to support, we first reviewed relevant international standards. The results of this research can be seen in the table below[1]. Relevant positions of the standards are referenced. The compatibility of those mechanisms with the presented approach will be discussed in the next paragraphs of this paper.

Table 1. Software Safety Mechanisms in International Standards.

Name/Description	Standards
Error detection codes	IEC 61508–3 (C.3.2)
	ISO 26262–6 (Table 4/5)
	ISO 26262–10 (Table A.5)
Watchdog mechanism	ISO 26262–6 (Table 4)
Range checks for input and output data	ISO 26262–6 (Table 4)
Plausibility check	ISO 26262–6 (Table 4)
Detection of data errors	ISO 26262–6 (Table 4)
External monitoring facility	IEC 61508–3 (Table A.2)
	ISO 26262–6 (Table 4)
Majority voter	IEC 61508–7 (A.1.4)
	ISO 26262–5 (Table D.2)
Control flow monitoring	ISO 26262–6 (Table 4)
Static recovery mechanism	ISO 26262–6 (Table 5)
Self-test by software	IEC 61508–2 (A.3.2)
	ISO 26262–5 (D.2.3.3)
Graceful degradation	IEC 61508–3 (C.3.8)
	ISO 26262–6 (Table 5)
Independent parallel redundancy	ISO 26262–6 (Table 5)

For the proof-of-concept implementation of this work, we implemented three custom software safety mechanisms that cover a larger part of Table 1.

Contracts. This software safety mechanism is based on the Design by Contract programming paradigm [13]. It can be used to perform checks on the input and output variables of function calls in the form of assumptions and guarantees. If the calling party fulfills the assumption of the contract, the function itself is obligated to meet the guarantee. When the guarantee isn't satisfied, the function itself is to blame. If the assumption is not met, it is the fault of the calling party. This approach of using contracts for runtime monitoring in C++ was already published by us in [14]. Contracts can be utilized to perform range checks of input and output data or plausibility checks as requested by safety standards (see Table 1).

Dual Modular Redundancy. The dual modular redundancy (DMR) mechanism can be applied to function calls. If applied, the function is executed redundantly. The results of both executions are then passed to redundant voter components. If the results match, there is no error. If there is a discrepancy, an appropriate error handling will be initiated. The DMR mechanism can be used

---

[1] Result of the SAFE4I project (01IS17032L).

for the detection of data errors, having a majority voter or as an external monitoring facility.

Time Measurement and Control Blocks. In addition, a software safety mechanism for analyzing, altering or monitoring the timing behavior of an application has been implemented. It covers the watchdog functionality listed in Table 1. The implementation is based on the work of Bruns et al. [6]. The mechanism is used for analysis purposes by measuring the execution time of a specific program section. In addition, the mechanism can also ensure that a specified execution time is not exceeded or it even allows to enforce a desired execution time by forcing a program section to consume all of its specified time. This can be helpful, e.g., if the environment expects a certain temporal behavior from the application.

3   Approach

In this section we describe our proposed approach for the semi-automated integration of software safety mechanisms. The overall process of the approach is depicted in Fig. 2. The actual integration of software safety mechanisms happens as a source-to-source transformation where existing functional source code is systematically extended by calls to software safety mechanism libraries. Possible integration points for mechanisms are found automatically by analyzing the functional source code.

3.1   Prerequisites

In order for this source-to-source transformation to take place, the following preconditions must be met. For one, the functional source code must be available for analysis and rewriting. Furthermore, software safety mechanisms (SSM) must be implemented in a specific library-based manner and be accompanied by a model representation, called `SSM Model`. This representation contains, among other things, necessary information for the actual code changes during integration and allows for formulating requirements of the software safety mechanism to the hardware/software environment. In order to check requirements automatically during the integration process, the target platform has to be modelled accordingly. The modelling process is called `Target2Model` and the resulting model is labeled as `Target Platform Model`. Both can be seen in the upper right part of Fig. 2. They are depicted somewhat transparently since there is no direct contribution to this part described in this paper.

3.2   Process

The process starts with automatically analyzing the functional source code to find all possible integration points for software safety mechanisms. The result of this analysis is the `Application Model`. The analysis itself is called `Code2Model` and is numbered as 1 in Fig. 2. A detailed description of the model and its automatic generation is provided in Subsect. 3.3. Within a graphical user interface, the safety engineer is now able to map available and compatible software safety mechanisms to integration points. The `SSM Model` of the mechanism defines what type of integration points are viable options. In addition, requirements that the mechanisms have of the target platform will be checked automatically against the `Target Platform Model`. Also, if the general functionality of the software safety mechanism allows it, parts of the mechanism can be mapped to hardware/software resources via configuration. The mapping of a `SSM Model` to the `Application`- and the `Target Platform Model` is referred to as `Weaving` while the required manual configuration by a safety engineer is labeled as `Setup` in Fig. 2. The result of the mapping is labeled as `Final Model`. It contains all necessary information to rewrite and thereby safeguard the functional source code.

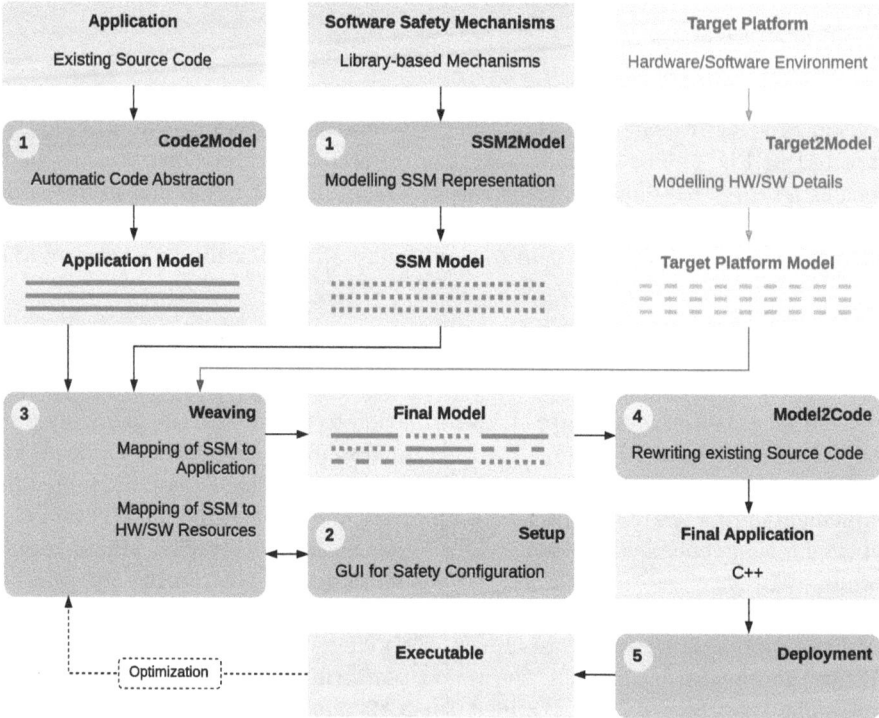

Fig. 2. Overview of the Approach

The source code rewriting is called `Model2Code` in the overview figure. Based on the previously generated model, calls to software safety mechanism libraries are written to integration points in the functional source code. Depending on the implementation of the mechanism, possible dependencies in the linking step may need to be resolved. Otherwise, the deployment will happen as usual.

3.3   Application Model

The `Application Model` serves to hold all information about the functional source code required by the integration process. We determined the necessary information on the basis of the previously identified software safety mechanisms found in standards, listed in Table 1. Furthermore, the `Application Model` is used for the visual abstraction of the functional source code, which the safety engineer uses to determine where software safety mechanisms should be integrated. For this reason, the control flow is part of the model since it supports the decision-making, for example, as to what parts of the application should potentially be executed redundantly or where a watchdog mechanism should sensibly enforce timing constraints.

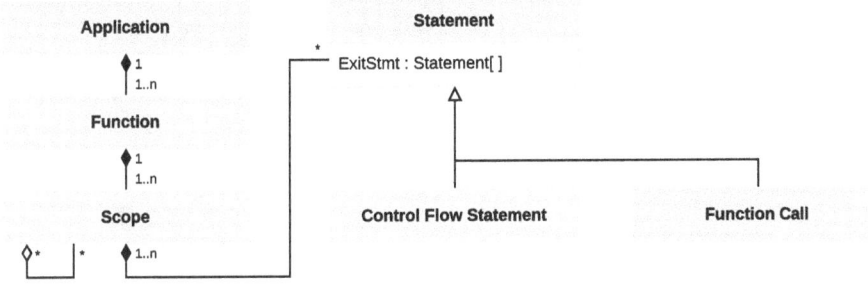

Fig. 3. Application Meta Model

Figure 3 shows the meta model of the `Application Model`. An abstraction of the functional source code happens function-wise. In functions there are scopes, which in turn can contain further scopes. Inside those scopes can be function calls or control flow changing statements. Both have a common parent class, that holds an adjacency list to store the actual control flow between statements. As of now, two ways of integration points are supported. Mechanisms can be applied to scopes and/or to function calls.

Automatic Code Abstraction. The automatic abstraction of the functional source code happens in the `Code2Model` step of Fig. 2. At first, the abstract syntax tree (AST) of the code is generated. Integration points are then extracted from the AST with the help of AST matchers. In order to gather the control flow between the integration points, a source-level, intra-procedural control flow graph is generated. Combined, these aspects form the `Application Model`.

4   Demonstration

Proof-of-Concept Implementation. We carried out a proof-of-concept implementation to evaluate the concepts developed within this work. Tools for abstracting and rewriting the functional source code were created on the basis of

Clang LibTooling [5]. The AST Matching was realized with [2], the source-level control flow graph was created with [3]. Also, we created a user interface as a Visual Studio Code extension. The example Application Models in the images below are actually screenshots from this extension. The source code rewriting was realized with [4].

Adaptive Cruise Control Example. The proposed method is demonstrated using source code excerpts from a simplified adaptive cruise control (ACC) system. In particular, the function for updating the speed is considered. For the demonstration, this chapter first describes a functional source code snippet of the ACC and then shows the visual representation of the corresponding Application Model. The actual changes in the C++ source code caused by the integration of software safety mechanisms are described later.

The left side of Fig. 4 shows the Update function. First, the control deviation for the PID controller is calculated, which is then passed to the PID_calculate function. The result of this function is the speed adjustment. A conditional statement checks whether the new speed value would fall below a threshold value. If so, the function DisableACC would deactivate the system. Otherwise, the SetSpeed function passes on the new speed value to the actuating system.

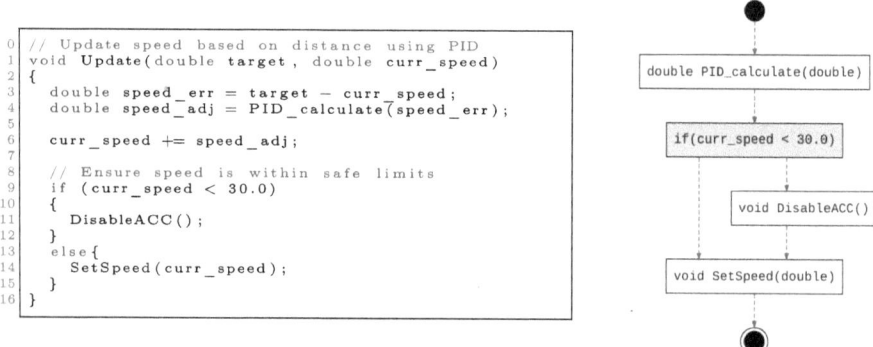

```
0   // Update speed based on distance using PID
1   void Update(double target, double curr_speed)
2   {
3       double speed_err = target - curr_speed;
4       double speed_adj = PID_calculate(speed_err);
5
6       curr_speed += speed_adj;
7
8       // Ensure speed is within safe limits
9       if (curr_speed < 30.0)
10      {
11          DisableACC();
12      }
13      else {
14          SetSpeed(curr_speed);
15      }
16  }
```

Fig. 4. Functional Source Code and the Corresponding Visual Representation of the Application Model

The right side of Fig. 4 shows the visual representation of the Application Model. The white nodes are integrations points. The grey nodes represent control flow changing statements. The extensions user could select an integration point, whereupon the software safety mechanisms catalog is presented. If an edge is selected, all edges of the directly associated scope are highlighted, then the user can select compatible mechanisms.

The example safety setup will be as follows: The PID_calculate function will be safeguarded with a DMR mechanism, while a Time Measurement and Control Block will ensure that the maximum execution time of DisableACC is not exceeded. Finally, a Contract safety mechanism will be utilized to perform plausibility checks on the SetSpeed function.

The result of the automatic integration can be seen in Listing 1.1 and Fig. 5. Applying mechanisms to non member function calls is very straightforward. To do this, the original function call is simply replaced with a wrapper function. The wrapper function is defined in an additional header file (rg_config.hpp) which has to be included. It executes the software safety mechanism and the safeguarded function. This way, the perceived changes to the functional code will be kept to a minimum. The wrapper function has the original name, extended by a random suffix, as seen in line 6, 13 and 16. The source code generation for the wrapper function, the rewriting of the original function call and the include of the additional header file all happen automatically.

Applying mechanisms to member function calls is also possible, though it is somewhat more complex. It requires passing the member function call as a function object to the wrapper function using a lambda expression. After that, the procedure is the same.

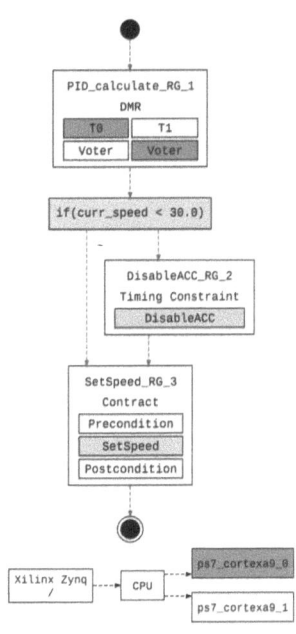

Fig. 5. Application and hardware model with applied mechanisms

```
0   #include "rg_config.hpp"
1
2   // Update speed based on distance
        using PID
3   void Update(double target, double
        curr_speed)
4   {
5       double speed_err = target -
            curr_speed;
6       double speed_adj =
            PID_calculate_RG_1(speed_err);
7
8       curr_speed += speed_adj;
9
10      // Ensure speed is within safe
            limits
11      if (current_speed < 30.0)
12      {
13          DisableACC_RG_2();
14      }
15      else{
16          SetSpeed_RG_3(curr_speed);
17      }
18  }
```

Listing 1.1. Functional code after Weaving

Listing 1.2 shows the wrapper functions. If a software safety mechanism is used, the necessary library includes (line 0 to 2) and function definitions (line 4 to 6) are added to the header file. Also, the boiler plate code for the respective mechanisms are automatically generated and added. In the case of the DMR mechanism (PID_calculate_RG_1), source code lines 8 to 18 were generated. Lines 13 to 16 define the mapping to the hardware. Default values are initially entered here, which must be configured accordingly by a safety engineer. Figure 5 shows how the tooling visually indicates the configured mapping through color coding.

DisableACC_RG_2 shows the application of the Time Measurement and Control Block. In line 24 the constructor of MaxExecutionTime is called and the met object is created. This starts a monitoring thread that ensures a maximum execution time. The wrapper function for the Contract mechanism had to be omitted due to the limited page length.

```
0  #include <dmr.hpp>
1  #include <timing_analysis.hpp>
2  #include <scontract.hpp>
3
4  double PID_calculate(double error);
5  void DisableACC();
6  void SetSpeed(double speed);
7
8  // RG 1
9  // --------------------------------------------------
10 inline double PID_calculate_RG_1(double error)
11 {
12    auto d = DTMR(f);
13    d.MapT0To(CPU::ps7_cortexa9_0);
14    d.MapT1To(CPU::ps7_cortexa9_1);
15    d.MapVoter0To(CPU::ps7_cortexa9_1);
16    d.MapVoter1To(CPU::ps7_cortexa9_0);
17    return d.Execute(error);
18 }
19
20 // RG 2
21 // --------------------------------------------------
22 void DisableACC_RG_2()
23 {
24    auto met = MaxExecutionTime(2, std::chrono::milliseconds(10));
25    DisableACC();
26 }
```

Listing 1.2. Function wrapper for the DMR mechansim in rg_config.hpp

5   Related Work

This section first examines related work in general before focusing on aspect-oriented programming and respective approaches.

One related approach that generally aims to separate the concerns safety and functionality is the Universal Safety Format (USF) [8,9]. USF supports a model-driven development approach to automatically integrate software safety mechanisms into functional software. USF provides a domain-agnostic metamodel to describe the functional software as well as a transformation language, the USF Transformation Language (UTL), which is capable of incorporating mechanisms at model level. To bridge the gap between the domain-agnostic USF/UTL and the obviously domain-specific target system, appropriate tooling is necessary. The approach presented in this paper should be seen as complementary and compatible with USF since the tooling described in this paper could be used to apply the domain-agnostic methods of USF to a domain-specific purpose. The main focus of USF lies on the metamodel and the respective model transformations and not on the automated abstraction of existing source code or on the code rewriting/code generation process. Therefore, these two approaches complement each other.

Aspect-oriented programming (AOP) [12] is a programming paradigm that follows similar objectives to the approach presented here. It allows developers to modularize cross-cutting concerns, such as logging or error handling, which would otherwise span multiple modules. AOP separates these concerns from the main codebase and promises cleaner source code. Although AOP has several advantages, it has not yet established itself in hardware-oriented programming in C/C++, despite efforts to do so [1]. An exhaustive consideration of the applicability of AOP to safety-relevant systems is beyond the scope of this paper. Still, we will briefly discuss the relation to the ideas of this work. The approach presented in this paper is highly related to AOP. However, the complexity is reduced compared to AOP due to the limited integration points for mechanisms, though this also weakens the general ability to integrate source code into existing code bases. For the development of safety-relevant systems, the presented approach offers a better balance between complexity and effectiveness. The key difference from AOP is the combined, holistic view of functional source code, software safety mechanisms, and the targeted hardware/software environment.

One approach that tries to address the matter of cross-cutting concerns in embedded systems with the help of AOP can be found in [15]. Wehrmeister et al. present a model-driven engineering approach that combines the unified modeling language (UML) and AOP to improve encapsulation of concerns and speed up the development process. The authors' concept starts with a high-level system specification in UML, which is extended by additional diagrams to allow special modeling for AOP. In addition, this work uses a predefined set of aspects, which includes reusable model and source code elements for extra-functional requirements. During the modeling phase, these aspects can be applied to parts of the functional model. Afterward, a script-based generation tool will generate platform-specific source code. Model integration of aspects is not a part of this approach. Moreover, the development process of this approach begins with a modeling phase. The approach presented in this paper can be applied to existing code bases.

6   Conclusion and Future Work

In this paper, we presented a model-based approach that utilizes a strict separation between functional and safety software to automatically integrate software safety mechanisms into functional source code. A proof-of-concept implementation showcased the automatic analysis of functional source code for finding possible integration points and demonstrated the source code rewriting.

It should be noted that the procedure currently supports two types of integration points—both the automatic functional code analysis and the mechanisms implementations are tailored to this. This is, therefore, a limitation of the approach presented. However, this can be mitigated as follows: We consider the mechanisms required by the standards to be generally compatible. Section 2.2 already pointed out that the mechanisms of this paper already cover a significant part of Table 1. On the other hand, certain mechanisms will be too application-specific to benefit from a library-based approach. This applies, for instance, to the self-test, the static recovery, or the graceful degradation mechanism. Further experiments shall be carried out on this matter.

In addition, alternatives to the abstraction of functional software are to be studied in the future. A query-like approach, similar to that known from AOP, may be a beneficial extension to the approach. We expect that the presented approach will prove to be particularly useful in two use cases: the preservation of timing behavior of an application when retrofitting software safety mechanisms and the creation of software tests for existing applications. Both will be investigated in further studies. Moreover, a future evaluation will examine the functional integrity after weaving, the effectiveness of the software safety mechanisms, their resource usage, and the overall applicability of the approach.

Acknowledgments. This work was partially funded by the German Ministry of Education and Research (BMBF) (grant number 01IS17032L).

Disclosure of Interests. The authors have no competing interests to declare that are relevant to the content of this article.

References

1. Aspectc++. https://www.aspectc.org/
2. Ast-matcher. https://clang.llvm.org/docs/LibASTMatchersReference.html
3. Clang cfg. https://clang.llvm.org/doxygen/classclang_1_1CFG.html
4. clang::rewriter. https://clang.llvm.org/doxygen/classclang_1_1Rewriter.html
5. Libtooling. https://clang.llvm.org/docs/LibTooling.html
6. Bruns, F., Yarza, I., Ittershagen, P., Grüttner, K.: Time measurement and control blocks for bare-metal c++ applications. ACM Trans. Embedded Comput. Syst. **20** (6 2021). https://doi.org/10.1145/3434401
7. DO-178C: Software considerations in airborne systems and equipment certification. Standard, RTCA, Inc. and EUROCAE (2012)
8. Haxel, F., et al.: Universal safety format: Automated safety software generation. In: International Conference on Model-Driven Engineering and Software Development (2022). https://doi.org/10.5220/0010784200003119
9. Haxel, F., et al.: The universal safety format in action: Tool integration and practical application. SN Comput. Sci. **4** (2023). https://doi.org/10.1007/S42979-022-01532-Z
10. IEC61508: Functional safety of electrical/electronic/programmable electronic safety-related systems (e/e/pe, or e/e/pes). Standard, The International Electrotechnical Commission, Geneva, CH (2010)
11. ISO26262: Road vehicles - functional safety. Standard, International Organization for Standardization, Geneva, CH (2018)
12. Kiczales, G., et al.: Aspect-oriented programming. Lecture Notes in Computer Science (including subseries Lecture Notes in Artificial Intelligence and Lecture Notes in Bioinformatics) **1241**, 220–242 (1997). https://doi.org/10.1007/BFB0053381
13. Meyer, B.: Applying "design by contract". Computer **25**, 40–51 (1992). https://doi.org/10.1109/2.161279
14. Schmedes, R., Ittershagen, P., Grüttner, K.: Towards distributed runtime monitoring with c++ contracts (2019). https://doi.org/10.1145/3312614.3312645
15. Wehrmeister, M.A., et al.: Aspect-oriented model-driven engineering for embedded systems applied to automation systems. IEEE Trans. Industr. Inf. **9**, 2373–2386 (2013). https://doi.org/10.1109/TII.2013.2240308

An Architecture for Maintainable Multi-Client Multi-Device Remote User Interfaces

Tim Schattkowsky$^{(\boxtimes)}$ and Kathleen Strodick

Hamm-Lippstadt University of Applied Sciences, Lippstadt, Germany
{tim.schattkowsky,kathleen.strodick}@hshl.de

Abstract. Providing and maintaining lightweight graphical user interfaces for embedded devices is becoming an increasing burden. In particular, the commonly applied Web-interfaces usually require continuous maintenance during the product life cycle to keep up with changes in browser clients. Furthermore, in many application scenarios, like building automation, smart homes or smart factories, large numbers of embedded devices must be controlled and maintained through multiple remote user terminals that provide composite user interfaces for multiple devices (e.g., all actors in a hotel room). In this paper, we present an architecture for lightweight graphical user interfaces for embedded devices in which all presentation aspects, such as control layout and appearance, are completely defined and implemented by the clients. The embedded device only implements the presentation-independent core functionality of UI controls in terms of state changes in response to client events. As a result, different client implementations can directly connect to these controls and provide individual implementations of the complete presentation, including the capability to combine UI elements from various devices into a single user interface.

Keywords: Remote User Interfaces · Embedded Devices · IoT

1 Introduction

There are many application scenarios in which multiple networked embedded devices (e.g., actors and sensors) are installed in a project next to each other without further orchestration, but still require a common user interface (or even multiple) to control these devices from one location. An example may be home or building automation, where various actors and sensor related to lighting, HVAC, etc. exist and it is convenient to control some or all of them through respective user terminals. This may be a touch-screen for controlling all of the lighting in the conference room or a Web interface for controlling the entire building. Similar scenarios also occur when controlling devices on a production line. It is also quite common, that the same device function is controlled through multiple UIs and presented in different ways. However, many devices nowadays do not provide a simple or just consistent way to be integrated into such UIs and accessed by multiple clients. Beyond integration, many embedded devices need to provide UIs device configuration and maintenance that have to be maintained (e.g., browser compatibility) as well.

© IFIP International Federation for Information Processing 2026
Published by Springer Nature Switzerland AG 2026
M. A. Wehrmeister et al. (Eds.): IESS 2024, IFIP AICT 760, pp. 15–24, 2026.
https://doi.org/10.1007/978-3-032-07102-6_2

Since physical access to embedded devices is sometimes not convenient or even feasible (e.g., for devices mounted on a façade or underwater), the user interface is often provided through remote access to the device, usually via network. In such a scenario, the user interface itself is usually Web-based and can be accessed through a regular Web browser or a respective control embedded in an application.

Implementing Web-based user interfaces in an embedded device is often a painful process, in particular when limited resources also constrain the use of available frameworks. Thus, implementations are often quite proprietary and hard to maintain. However, since Web technologies and browsers evolve fast, any Web application including such a Web-based user interface needs to be constantly maintained to ensure compatibility with clients. In the case of an embedded device, this means not only continuous development efforts, but also the need to provide continuous updates to the devices installed in the field, where each installed device needs to be updated. While this is already an issue for desktop computers with constant internet connection, it can become impractical for embedded devices installed in the field.

In this paper, we propose an architecture for lightweight graphical user interfaces for embedded devices that enables multi-client remote user interfaces spanning multiple devices with minimal implementation effort on the embedded device. These interfaces are externally maintained, eliminating the need to update the device firmware to address issues like browser compatibility.

2   Related Work

In the development of interfaces for web applications, especially for mobile devices, several approaches and technologies have emerged to overcome the challenges of creating user-friendly and adaptable interfaces.

XML-based approaches have an important role to play in the development of Graphical User Interfaces (GUIs) for mobile devices. These methods offer flexibility and platform independence. XML (eXtensible Markup Language) provides a structured way to define the elements and layout of graphical user interfaces, which can then be rendered on different devices [18].

One example is the XML User Interface Language (XUL), which was developed by Mozilla. XUL simplifies the creation of cross-platform web applications with a consistent user interface by using XML to define widgets, layouts and event handlers [9]. Although initially popular, the use of XUL has declined due to the emergence of more modern frameworks.

The User Interface Markup Language (UIML) offers a more generalized approach that enables the description of user interfaces regardless of the target platform. UIML separates the structure, behavior and presentation of the interface and allows developers to create customizable interfaces. Nevertheless, the need for separate specifications for each platform remains a challenge [6, 8].

More advanced XML-based solutions include the eXtensible Interface Markup Language (XIML) and the User Interface Extensible Markup Language (UsiXML). XIML provides a framework for describing user interfaces on different abstraction levels, from high-level interaction models to particular implementation details [4]. UsiXML, on the other hand, focuses on model-driven development and enables the automatic generation of user interfaces from high-level models. These approaches allow developers to create interfaces that can be easily adapted to different device features and user preferences [7, 12].

YAML (YAML Ain't Markup Language) is a human-readable data serialization standard that is widely used for configuration files and data sharing between languages with differing data structures. Its simplicity and readability make it suitable for specifying setups and settings in web and mobile applications. Unlike XML, which may be very large and complex, YAML has a clear and simple syntax that makes it easier for developers to construct and manage configuration files [2, 14].

JSON is a data exchange format that is easy for humans to read and write and easy for machines to analyze and generate. JSON is often used in web applications for transferring data between a server and a client. Its compatibility with JavaScript makes it particularly suitable for web development. The JSON syntax is derived from JavaScript object notation and uses an intuitive and easy to use key-value pair format [10].

Although MQTT (Message Queuing Telemetry Transport) is not directly related to the development of user interfaces, it is an important component of the Internet of Things (IoT), which often includes web interfaces for device monitoring and control. MQTT is a publish-subscribe messaging protocol designed for resource-limited devices and networks with low bandwidth, high latency, or unreliability. Its high efficiency makes it ideal for mobile applications that need to communicate with IoT devices or backend services [11, 17]. The MQTT architecture consists of clients and a broker. Clients can publish or subscribe to messages on specific topics to receive them. The broker manages the distribution of messages to the appropriate clients. This separation of news producers and consumers allows for more scalable and flexible communication patterns [1]. MQTT can be used in combination with web interfaces to provide real-time dashboards and control panels for IoT applications. For example, a web-based Smart-Home application can use MQTT to receive sensor data and transmit control commands to devices such as lights and thermostats. MQTT ensures that the web interface remains responsive even when network resources are limited [15].

SLMP (SeamLess Message Protocol), developed by Mitsubishi Electric, is a protocol used in industrial automation for communication between Programmable Logic Controllers (PLCs) and other devices. Although SLMP is primarily used in industrial environments, it can also be useful in web interface contexts where real-time data from industrial equipment needs to be displayed or controlled via web applications. SLMP supports various communication patterns, including cyclic data exchange, transient message communication and file transfer. This versatility makes SLMP suitable for a wide range of industrial applications, from simple monitoring tasks to complex control systems [13]. The integration of SLMP into web interfaces enables the creation of sophisticated industrial control panels that can be accessed from any web browser. For example, a web-based SCADA (Supervisory Control and Data Acquisition) system can use SLMP to monitor and control factory equipment and provide operators with real-time data and control functions. This integration improves the usability and accessibility of industrial automation systems [3].

RDM (Remote Device Management) is an extension of the DMX512 protocol used in entertainment lighting. It enables bidirectional communication between lighting controllers and spotlights. In the context of web interfaces, RDM can be used to create web-based lighting control systems where the interface needs to both send commands to and receive status updates from lighting devices. RDM enables functions such as remote configuration, status monitoring and diagnostics of lighting fixtures. This function is particularly valuable for large lighting installations where manual configuration and monitoring would be impractical. Web interfaces that utilize RDM provide lighting designers and operators with intuitive control panels that can be accessed from any device with a web browser. These interfaces can display real-time status information such as device settings, error messages and performance metrics. In addition, operators can use the web interface to adjust lighting parameters, create lighting scenes and schedule events - all from one centralized location [5, 16].

3 Basic Architecture

As shown in Fig. 1, our architecture separates the presentation and logic of the UI controls between the UI client and the embedded device, which acts as the server for all connected UI clients. Multiple UI clients can connect to the same embedded device via network and offer the same control in different user interfaces with different client-side implementations (e.g., native vs. Web-based). Thus, maintenance on the presentation side can be done without the need to maintain devices in the field (i.e., update device firmware). Furthermore, this separation enables incorporating the same control (e.g., for the temperature of an AC system) in multiple client UIs in different ways.

This differs from the usual separation of user interface and application logic in that we physically separate the presentation and logic of the individual controls. This means that for each UI element, such as a button, an edit field, or simply a label, the basic functionality (i.e., the state changes in response to user input and programmatic changes on the device side) is implemented by the embedded device and wired to the application logic. While the UI client provides an implementation of the controls appearance that reflects the state information provided by the embedded device. Thus, the UI client implementation can be individually maintained as needed and the same control for a device can have different presentations and on different clients.

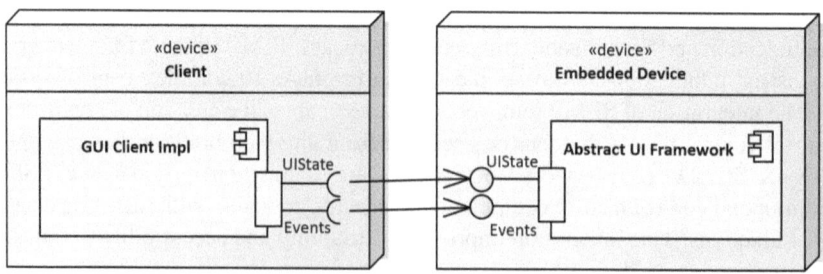

Fig. 1. Remote UI Architecture

The embedded device provides a basic implementation of all supported UI elements of the Abstract UI framework. These controls reflect state information corresponding to their respective type and can respond to programmatic and user input events, but have no notion of presentation. As an example, the implementation of a choice control for picking an item from a list is aware of the selection options and the selected item, but has no information regarding presentation aspects such as positioning or colors.

On the embedded device, the Abstract UI controls are integrated into the code as usual, except that the code no longer controls the layout or appearance of the controls, making them smaller and simpler. Since the presentation is fully implemented on the UI client side, this approach eliminates the need to update the device firmware to fix issues like browser compatibility.

The UI client not only implements the presentation side of the Abstract UI framework's controls, but it additionally provides all other features of the user interface, such as a layout concept and the construction of fundamental UI elements. This can be done in various ways from a Web-application to a native client. Different implementations can still be connected to the same device and controller.

The state of the client UI is completely determined by the state information provided by the Abstract UI framework of the controlled device. The UI client does this by frequently polling the device's state changes. Such state changes happen when either a user interaction on a UI client generated an event notification (e.g., button press) to be communicated to the respective Abstract UI control implementation, or the embedded device's software manipulates the control directly, creating a state change in the control.

A typical UI client is likely to have access to a UI specification defining the complete UI. Depending on the application scenario, this UI may be defined in the context of just a single device, e.g., as the devices operation or maintenance UI, or it may cover multiple devices, e.g., to control all lights in a hotel suite. In the first case, the UI description can be stored on the embedded device itself and the UI client implementation can be fetched from the device or a Web location in response to accessing the device through a browser. However, in this scenario, the maintenance benefit might not exist as the client implementation is de-facto still stored on the device. However, multi-device UIs are likely to be defined externally anyway and are not affected by this consideration. This is the intended basis for the creation of a generic external editor for remote user interfaces that can be used both for the creation and maintenance of device UIs and for the creation of composite UIs in projects that span multiple devices, such as a production line or building level.

The Abstract UI Framework implements the embedded device side of the controls including the actual logic and the connection between the controls and their presentation counterpart in the UI client. For this, the framework provides state information for individual clients, and responds to client events by updating the UI state.

As the devices only provide individual controls for a UI, but not a complete UI including layout and presentation, it is useful to be able to query devices for the provided set or controls. This also allows generic clients or mechanisms to automatically generate initial UIs for a device. For this, the Abstract UI framework also provides a description of the available controls that can be obtained by any UI client.

4 Abstract UI Framework

The Abstract UI framework enables an embedded device to provide a remote user interface to compatible clients, while handling only the state relevant part of the user interface. For this, a set of abstract user interface elements is defined corresponding to the most common controls in user interfaces (e.g., buttons, sliders and edit fields). These UI elements respond to client events and programmatic manipulation on the embedded device and reflect their corresponding state directly to the embedded software and over network to all connected clients. For this, a HTTP/REST interface is used with JSON for describing UI element states and events.

4.1 Basic Model

The abstract UI elements expose their state through a set of attributes and change their state in response to events from the client UI (see Fig. 2). Furthermore, the embedded software can directly manipulate the controls by accessing their Attributes. This usually corresponds to setting the value represented by the control or controlling visibility and access to the control. UUIDs are employed to identify element types and their instances in the network communication and referencing the in the employed JSON objects.

The different supported Attribute types need separate implementations as these must be able to parse the corresponding text from the JSON objects and provide type-correct information to the surrounding embedded software. Also, implementing the Attributes as separate objects removes the need to have a reflection mechanism for accessing attributes directly on the UIElements, which simplifies implementation and is also a performance advantage.

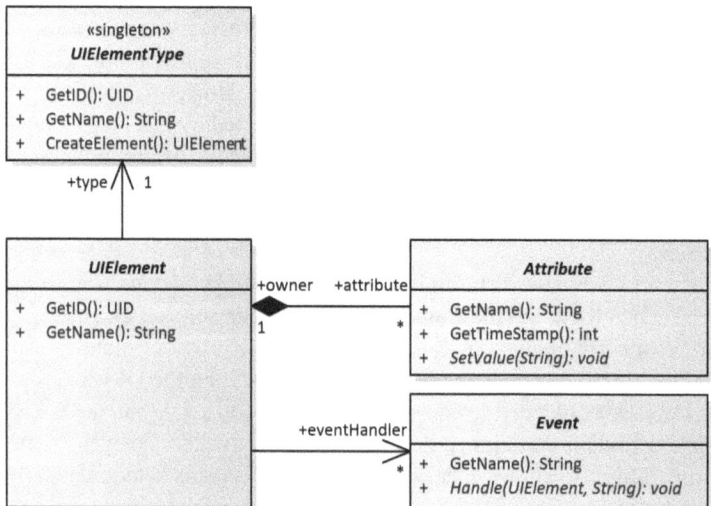

Fig. 2. Core Abstract UI Element Model

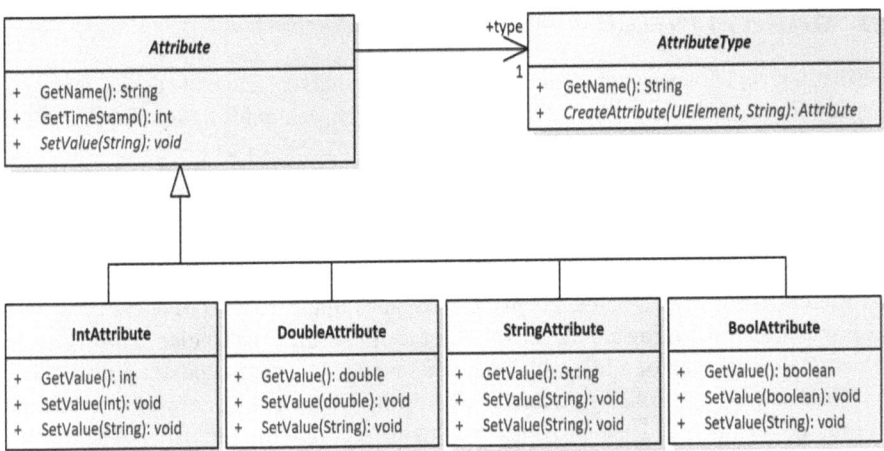

Fig. 3. Primitive Attribute Types

Figure 3 shows the supported primitive Attribute types, which just correspond to the most commonly used basic primitive types: 32-Bit integer, double precision floating point number, Boolean value, and UTF-8 Strings of up to 255 bytes.

Supporting also lower precision numbers would mainly increase implementation overhead. UTF-8 seems to be the most effective and well-supported text encoding. Limiting it to 255 bytes simplifies embedded memory management.

Beyond the primitive attribute types, we also support array as attribute types These are essentially handled in the same way, but their implementation allows clients to limit access to ranges only in order to avoid transferring unneeded data, like in the case of a list or text control that displays just a limited number of lines from the actual dataset. This will be further elaborated in Subsect. 4.2. However, currently array attributes are only employed for displaying data, but could be useful also for a text editor control.

All input data validation happens at the server. Thus, UI clients do not need to offer any validation mechanism for data provided via events. Once a value is sent to the server, the server UIElement will either accept the value through its SetValue(string) member and update its state accordingly, or it will implicitly reject the value by not changing its state. A UI client should track the state of an attribute value (see Fig. 4) and may additionally visually display that value state in the control to provide user feedback if the value has been applied.

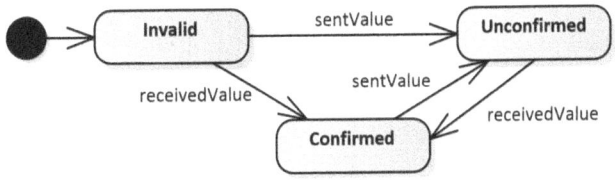

Fig. 4. Client-Side Attribute Value States

4.2 Abstract UI Elements

We distinguish between Input Controls that are intended to change the device state, and Display Controls that are only meant to display device state information. Input controls will send events (e.g., button press or value update) to the device in order to manipulate its state while display controls solely display updated state information from the device.

The set of input controls as shown in Fig. 5 includes the traditional basic set of controls. Besides the usual push- and toggle buttons, controls are here focused on their state alone. Thus, there is just one control to input every data type, that may be mapped to different control types on the client side. As an example, a slider or a text field could be employed for inputting an integer value at the client side. The Choice control enables selecting one item out of a list, which may be mapped to a combo box or a list view.

The list view control is particularly interesting because it has events to efficiently control the selection and also provides hints to the server to limit transferred state information. In this case, the implementation of the Selected and Options attributes will only provide values corresponding to the respective ClientState attributes, which are transferred to the server during for a state update request and there interpreted by the implementation of the corresponding attributes.

View controls (see Fig. 6) are primarily intended to display data of a certain type. Since the client-side formatting options depend on the actual data type, we provide corresponding view controls for all supported primitive data types and expand beyond that by enabling the explicit display of a color (e.g., for color selection or just to enable having a red warning light), the display of longer informational texts, a web page or a PNG or JPEG image. The latter can also be used to feed live as any state update that includes the image URL will cause the client to reload the image.

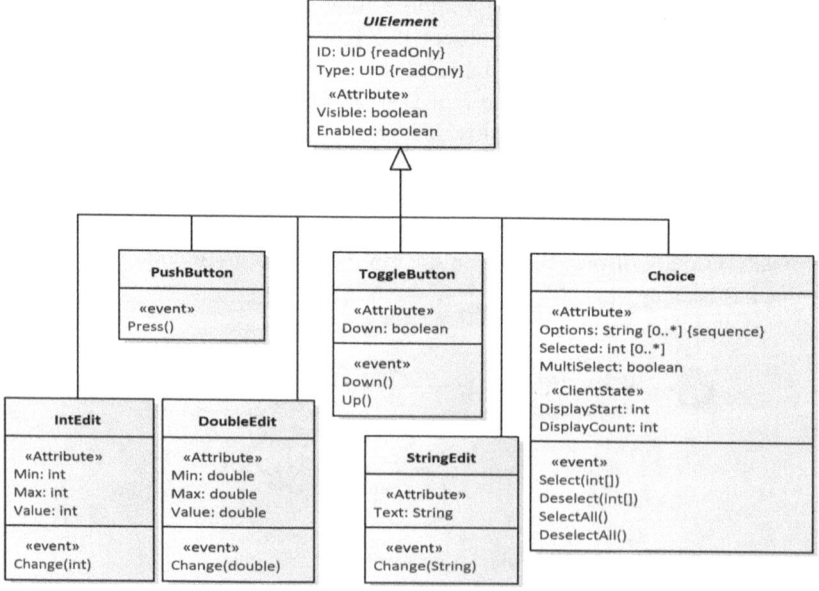

Fig. 5. Input Controls

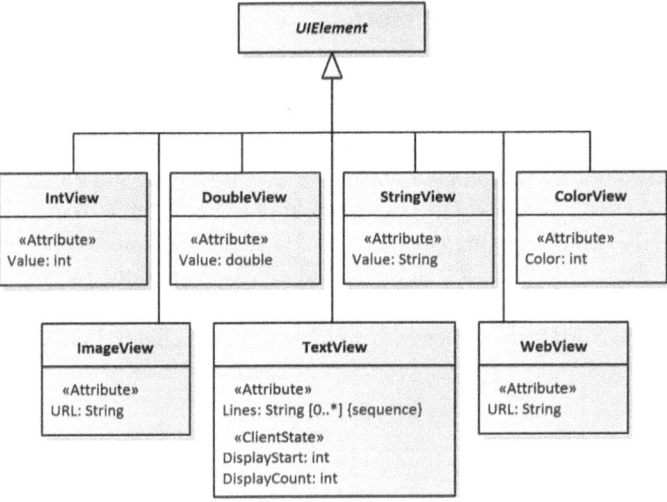

Fig. 6. View Controls

4.3 State Management

The Abstract UI framework on the embedded device (server) maintains state information for all UI Clients. State changes eventually correspond to attribute value changes on the server, which are tracked by the frameworks Attribute implementations. Each attribute holds a timestamp indicating the last value change. Thus, clients can poll value changes by indicating the timestamp of the last update and only receive changes since that update. The timestamp itself is incremented each time, a client receives an update set. Clients and server must be prepared for the timestamp to wraparound.

Clients poll state updates through an HTTP/REST interface. For this, the last known timestamp is provided in the URL while the request body contains the UUIDs of the controls monitored by the client and a UUID of the UI the client relates to. The latter is particularly relevant in case the server has changed the UI since the last request, e.g., because it is user-configurable. The server will provide a response including JSON objects describing all changed attributes on the respective UIElements identified by their UUID. The server may delay the response if no state change happened since the last update. However, the server must ensure that this does not block/delay the handling of subsequent events from the same client. This can be done using HTTP2, multiple connections or just through intelligent handling of pipelined requests.

4.4 Eventing

Events such as button presses are sent through the HTTP/REST interface of the server and dispatched to the corresponding UIElement identified in the respective URL. The request body includes again the UI UUID and a JSON object describing the event including event data such as a new value for an IntEdit. If an event changes the UI state, the affected Attributes are marked with the current time stamp. There is no need to increase the timestamp for events.

5   Conclusions and Future Work

We have presented an approach on lightweight remote graphical user interfaces that enables the external creation of multi-device multi-client user interfaces that can be independently maintained from the device firmware. This enables elements from various devices to be combined in a single user interface while having full control over layout and appearance of the controls. The framework has been implemented in various devices and is currently deployed using two different UI client implementations. Future work will include the development of a corresponding external editor for Web-based user interfaces that enables the creation of composite user interfaces for large projects like buildings or whole production lines with multiple different clients. Furthermore, we will investigate the scalability of the approach in scenarios with large numbers of devices and UI clients.

References

1. ANSI: Remote Device Management Over DMX512 Networks. ANSI E1.20 (2006)
2. Mackenzie, C.: YAML: a comprehensive guide to the configuration language. J. Softw. Eng. Appl. **12**(3), 123–134 (2018)
3. CC-Link Partner Association: SLMP. CC-Link Partner Association
4. Calvary, G., Vanderdonckt, J.: Extensible Interface Markup Language (XIML): concepts, technologies, and applications. Comput. Stand. Interfaces **25**, 131–140 (2003)
5. Choi, S.I., et al.: Reliable Transmission for RDM Protocol in Lighting Control Networks. In: Ubiquitous Information Technologies and Applications, 280. Springer (2014)
6. Goderis, S.: On the separation of user interface concerns: a programmer's perspective on the modularisation of user interface code. ASP/VUBPRESS/UPA, Antwerp (2008)
7. Guerrero, J., et al.: A theoretical survey of user interface description languages: complementary results. In: UsiXML 2011, pp. 229–236 (2011)
8. Harmonia Inc.: UIML: A device-independent User Interface Markup Language. In: Proceedings of the ACM Symposium on User Interface Software and Technology (1999)
9. Hyatt, D., Shaver, M.: XUL: a user interface markup language for network-centric applications. In: Proceedings of the 7th International World Wide Web Conference (1998)
10. Irshad, L., et al.: Schema-based JSON data stores in relational databases. J. Database Manage. (JDM) **30**(3), 38–70 (2019)
11. Johnson, B., Miller, C.: Secure Data Distribution Architecture in IoT Using MQTT. MDPI, 2023
12. Limbourg, Q., et al.: UsiXML: A Language Supporting Multi-Path Development of User Interfaces. In: Engineering HCI and Interactive Systems, pp. 200–220. Springer (2004)
13. Mitsubishi Electric Corporation: SLMP Reference Manual. Mitsubishi Electric (2023)
14. Ben-Kiki, O., et al.: YAML Ain't Markup Language Version 1.2. YAML.org (2009)
15. Pedreiras, P., Almeida, L.: Extending MQTT with real-time communication services based on SDN. Sensors **22**(9), 3162 (2022). https://doi.org/10.3390/s22093162
16. Samandari, J., Gritti, C.: Post-quantum authentication in the MQTT protocol. J. Cybersecurity Privacy **3**(3), 416–434 (2023). https://doi.org/10.3390/jcp3030021
17. Smith, J., Doe, A.: MQTT Protocol: Fundamentals and Directions. IEEE Xplore (2023)
18. Wimmer, M.K.: XML-based Technologies for the Generation of Adaptive User Interfaces in the Web. Springer (2004)

A High-Efficiency Dual-Channel Pixel Processor for Event-Based Camera

Zhaoqi Wang$^{(\boxtimes)}$ (iD), Miao He(iD), Yu Feng(iD), and Christophe Bobda(iD)

Department of Electrical and Computer Engineering, University of Florida,
Gainesville, FL, USA
`wangzhaoqi@ufl.edu`

Abstract. The increasing resolution of modern sensors results in significant data volumes and overwhelming communication links between images and back-end processors in embedded systems or the cloud. Event cameras mitigate this issue by reducing image data volume, thereby alleviating the pressure, but they necessitate the back-end processor to reconstruct the original image. We propose an advanced event camera system that integrates inference within the sensor itself, using an event-based mechanism to compute relevant pixels for knowledge inference. This pixel processing unit features a dual-channel filter with a Spatial *Saliency Generator Unit* (SSU), a *Temporal Saliency Generator Unit* (TSU), and a *Saliency Integrating Unit* (SIU), which determine salient pixels from current and previous frames. Compared to HARP [6], the FPGA implementation of this architecture significantly enhances computing efficiency and hardware utilization, achieving a 94.55% reduction in LUT usage, a 99.39% reduction in Flip-Flop usage, and a 29.63% reduction in BRAM usage.

Keywords: FPGA · Event Camera · Image Processing

1 Introduction

Machine learning and deep learning are disruptive technologies that have been increasingly applied across various research fields in recent years, even including environmental engineering [16], medical engineering [17,18], and others, where efficient deep learning applications are highly sought after. More and more researchers are applying machine learning and deep learning on a wide variety of equipment. As a result, there is a growing demand for deploying these algorithms on edge devices, which are resource-constrained environments. For video-processing tasks, one promising technology that aims to reduce power consumption and resource usage is the event camera.

Event cameras are bio-inspired vision sensors designed to generate image frames asynchronously based on scenic events [3]. Unlike conventional cameras, event cameras produce output only when a new event appears in their field of

Supported by University of Florida.

M. A. Wehrmeister et al. (Eds.): IESS 2024, IFIP AICT 760, pp. 25–35, 2026.
https://doi.org/10.1007/978-3-032-07102-6_3

view. There is a growing body of work on incorporating machine learning models into image sensors [4–6]. Research shows that processing the non-traditional data streams generated by these vision sensors requires new algorithms and methods to realize their full potential [10]. However, researchers face two major challenges: the available event cameras are insufficient in number, variety, and processing efficiency, and their cost is prohibitively high. Additionally, these cameras face limitations such as low resolution and limited configurability.

1.1 Motivation

It is becoming increasingly challenging to apply event cameras and deep learning applications on edge devices, such as traffic smart cameras [1,2,8], drones [7] and underwater robots [15], all of which require efficient deep learning architectures for practical deployment. However, AI applications and other tasks on these devices also demand substantial computing resources, making it particularly important to optimize computational efficiency on the sensor side [9]. Furthermore, the dynamic and often unpredictable environments in which these edge devices operate necessitate robust and adaptive vision sensors capable of real-time processing. Event cameras, with their ability to capture changes in a scene with minimal latency, offer a promising solution. However, their widespread adoption is hindered by several technical limitations, including high costs, low resolution, and limited configurability.

To address these challenges, innovative approaches are needed to integrate event cameras with resource-efficient deep learning models. This involves developing new algorithms that can leverage the unique data from event cameras while minimizing computational overhead. Optimizing hardware utilization is also essential to ensure these systems operate effectively within the constraints of edge devices.

The motivation for this research is twofold: to enhance the practicality of event cameras for edge applications by overcoming their current limitations, and to contribute to developing more sustainable AI-driven technologies. By focusing on reducing computational overhead and improving hardware efficiency, our research aims to bridge the gap between the high performance required for advanced vision tasks and the limited computing resources available on edge devices. The integration of FPGAs plays a crucial role, optimizing computational and hardware resources, and unlocking the full potential of event cameras.

Addressing these issues can improve the performance and computational efficiency of event cameras, potentially leading to broader adoption in fields such as traffic monitoring, autonomous driving, surveillance, and environmental monitoring.

1.2 Contribution

In this paper, we propose a novel high-performance dual-channel pixel processor unit for event cameras, aiming to address computing efficiency challenges and hardware utilization in resource-constrained edge devices. Our approach integrates spatial and temporal saliency detection to enhance the identification of significant events, and our design focuses on optimizing processing efficiency and hardware resource consumption. This paper develops a dual-channel filter design, *Pixel Processing Unit* (PPU), which includes *Spatial Saliency Generator Unit* (SSU), *Temporal Saliency Generator Unit* (TSU), and *Saliency Integration Unit* (SIU), to calculate the salient pixels in the current frame based on the current frame and the previous frame. Through this calculation method, the salient pixels in each frame of the real-time captured video signal can be calculated, providing significant information to enhance the efficiency of the subsequent machine learning module. The key contributions of our work are as follows:

– The methodology optimizes data flow to reduce DDR memory bandwidth consumption by using *Block RAM* (BRAM) for intermediate storage and processing. This approach enhances data throughput, minimizes delays in saliency calculations, improves hardware resources consumption, and speeds up processing. The use of *AXI Video Direct Memory Access* (AXI VDMA) for data transfers further synchronizes the PS and PL, boosting system performance.
– Our proposed pixel processing unit leverages LUTs and FFs more efficiently than event-based architecture presented in HARP [6] and Saliency Model applied in HMAX [12]. It also showcases a substantial reduction in hardware resource requirements and computational delay.

2   Related Works

2.1   Improvement for Event-Camera

Event cameras [3] have gained substantial popularity recently, particularly for their potential in edge devices where computing resources and power efficiency is crucial. Most people try to make some improvements by modifying the model or algorithm. Daniel Gehrig et al. [10] introduced an algorithm that utilizes a generative model based on photometric information, employing maximum likelihood to interpret events directly from the raw intensity measurements of frames. And it significantly improves the efficiency of event cameras.

2.2   Hardware Side Improvement for Event Camera

Unlike the previously mentioned model and algorithm methods, modifying the hardware architecture can significantly improve efficiency. The most common method is resizing, which can be broadly categorized into two approaches: one involves shrinking the frames, such as Mishra et al. [14] who use the cvResize() function to downscale images, concentrating the information into a smaller resolution. The alternative approach is to determine whether the pixels are salient. Park et al. [12] introduced a saliency model using a *Center-Surround Difference* (CSD) method, which calculates the difference between the value of the center pixel of each pixel and the value of its surrounding pixels at different scales. Bhowmik et al. [6] proposed *the Hierarchical Attention Oriented Region-Based Processing* (HARP) architecture, which employs a *Pixel Processing Unit* (PPU) and an *Attention Module* (AM) to calculate *Temporal and Spatial Saliency* (TS SS). They conducted numerous experiments to establish a threshold. If the difference between the center and neighbor pixel groups exceeds this threshold, the pixels are labeled as salient.

2.3   Innovation

By integrating methods from previous pixel processing modules, we have created a novel pixel processor that significantly reduces hardware resources while enhancing the ability to recognize smaller, more detailed objects. This is achieved by using individual pixel blocks as the smallest processing units, thereby improving the overall performance of event cameras. Additionally, we employ *Direct Memory Access* (DMA) technology to save computational power by transferring data between peripherals and DDR without CPU intervention.

3   Dual-Channel Processing Design

This section will first outline the fundamental principles behind the event camera we have developed. Following that, we will explain the design process and the architecture of the pixel processor unit.

3.1   Event Camera Architecture

Without lost of the generality in the generic organization of our design, the video processing system is based on the Xilinx Zynq-7000 SoC [13] architecture. The processing system (PS), also referred to as the software component, includes the ARM Cortex-A9 processor cores and handles the software tasks and general-purpose processing. The programming logic (PL), also known as the hardware component, consists of FPGA fabric and manages the hardware acceleration and specialized processing tasks. This design contains 64 pixel processing units (PPU)s working in parallel, further enhancing the system's ability to handle high-resolution video data and complex saliency calculations efficiently. A PPU (see Sect. 3.2) operates on a single pixel, using neighbours' values to produce the result of a transformation of that pixel.

As shown in Fig. 1, the processing logic operates as follows:

- Step 1 is to start up the system.
- Step 2 is to capture and transfer video frames
- Step 3 is to calculate the initial Saliency.
- Step 4 is ongoing Saliency calculation and data retrieval

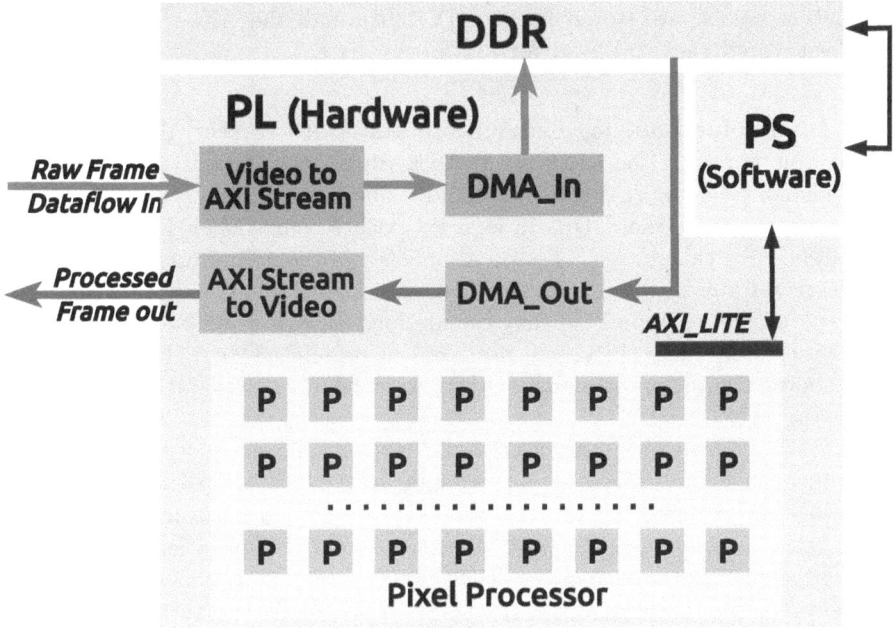

Fig. 1. Event Camera Architecture

Step 1: System Start Up. Upon system startup, the PS initializes the camera sensor, configures its operating mode and parameters via the IIC interface, sets up the AXI VDMA module, defines the frame buffer address and transmission parameters, and activates the Saliency calculation module. Additionally, the PS orchestrates the Saliency calculation process, ensuring synchronized operation of each module and managing data transmission within DDR [11] memory to guarantee proper storage and retrieval of video frame data and Saliency calculation results.

Step 2: Capture and Transfer Video Frames. Once a video frame is captured, the video signal is converted into an AXI4-Stream data stream by the Video to AXI Stream module as shown in Fig. 1 and sent to the AXI VDMA module. The AXI VDMA module then transfers the video frame data to the DDR memory through the AXI bus, with the entire process managed by the PS memory controller.

Step 3: Initial Saliency Calculation. The Saliency calculation module reads the first frame of video data from DDR through PS and caches it into the BRAM configured in each PPU through the AXI_LITE interface to improve access speed. The spatial Saliency calculation is performed in BRAM, and the calculation results are stored back to DDR through the AXI_LITE interface and then stored back to PS for further processing.

Step 4: Ongoing Saliency Calculation and Data Retrieval. As the camera module captures the subsequent video frame, the data is transmitted to DDR memory via the AXI VDMA module. The pixel processor module fetches the new frame data from DDR through PS, caches it into BRAM, and performs spatial Saliency calculations. Temporal Saliency is then determined by comparing the new frame with the previous one, with the results stored back in DDR. Both spatial and temporal Saliency calculations are processed by an array of 64 pixel processing units (PPU, see Sect. 3.2) in parallel. The AXI VDMA module retrieves the processed Saliency data from DDR in preparation for further processing.

While the current implementation focuses on efficient saliency calculation and processing, the processed data can be fed directly into the software for future advanced tasks. These tasks may include machine learning algorithms, *Deep Neural Networks* (DNN), and other sophisticated applications. This future integration ensures the system is efficient in its current operations and adaptable for more complex processing requirements in subsequent research. This paper focus is on the efficient implementation of the event camera part in a low-cost FPGA for the purpose of relevance-oriented data reduction.

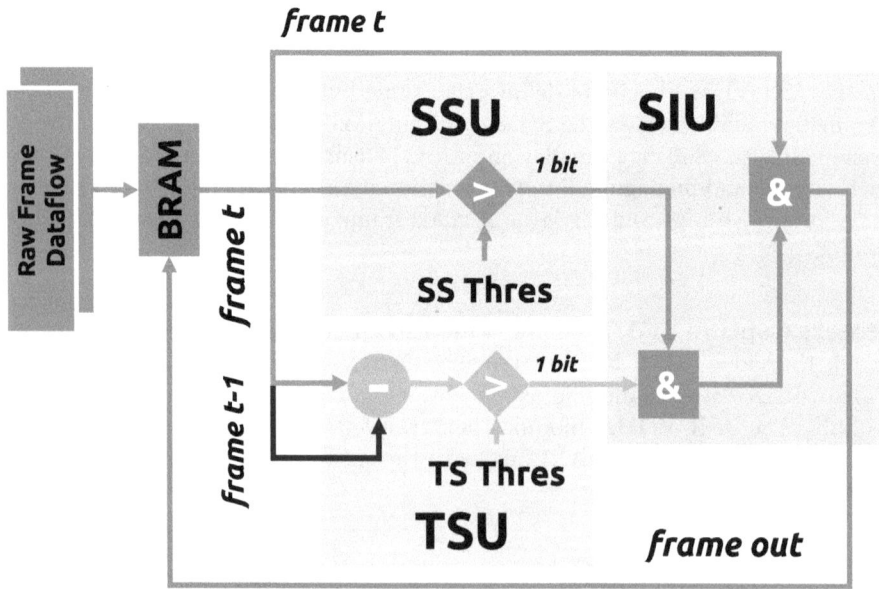

Fig. 2. Proposed Dual-Channel Workflow

3.2 Pixel Processing Unit

Each PPU contains a structure shown in Fig. 2, which consists of three main units: SSU, TSU, and SIU. A BRAM is also contained to assist in processing frame data and improve the processing speed of PPU.

The principle for the SSU is shown in Fig. 3. This unit performs an intra-frame comparison, where each frame comprises 640×480 pixels. These pixels are classified into two categories: edge pixels (those on all sides that have fewer than four adjacent pixels) and center pixels:

- For the edge pixels, it is assumed that significant events will not appear in these regions. Therefore, these pixels are directly labeled as 0.
- For the center pixels, the Unit compares the values of the three RGB channels of a pixel and its adjacent pixels, and their average values are calculated. Suppose the difference between the three channels exceeds a *Spatial Saliency threshold* (SsThreshold). In that case, it is considered that the difference between this pixel and the surrounding pixels is significant, and this pixel is marked as 1, indicating that the pixel is salient in spatial terms; otherwise, it is marked as 0.

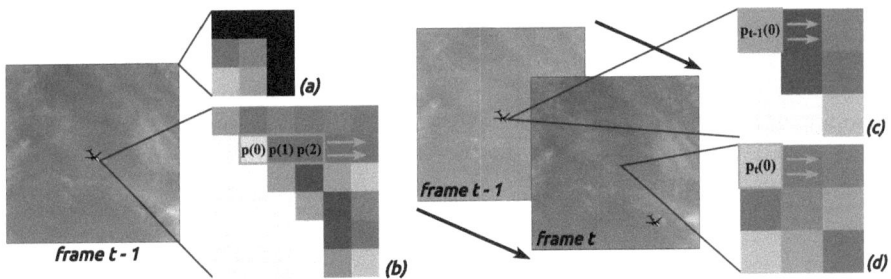

Fig. 3. SSU Processing (left) and TSU Processing (right)

The principle of the TSU is illustrated in Fig. 3. This unit performs an inter-frame comparison, with the minimum comparison unit being a pixel. However, unlike the SSU, it compares pixels across different frames.

- To obtain the TSU result, pixels from the current processing frame are compared with pixels at the same positions in the previous frame. Similar to the SSU comparison, the TSU evaluates the values of the three RGB channels of each pixel. If the difference in the three-channel values exceeds a predefined *Temporal Saliency threshold* (TsThreshold), the pixel is labeled as 1, indicating temporal Saliency. For the first frame, since there is no preceding frame for comparison, all pixels are directly labeled as 0.

The SIU operates as a two-layer AND logic unit to effectively combine *Spatial and Temporal Saliency* scores. The first layer, as shown in Table 1, processes the Spatial Saliency Score and the Temporal Saliency Score using AND logic to

Table 1. Event Based Saliency Generator Computation

SS Score	TS Score	Generated Saliency Score	Output
0	0	Inactive	Blank
0	1	Inactive	Blank
1	0	Inactive	Blank
1	1	**Active**	Pixel Data

generate a binary frame label matrix. Only the pixels that receive a score of 1 from both Saliency channels are marked as active. This matrix is a mask, with pixels of interest marked with 1 s and non-salient pixels marked with 0 s. In the second layer, the unit applies AND logic to the frame label matrix and the original frame, retaining the pixel data where the label is 1 and discarding the pixel data where the label is 0. This ensures that only the salient regions of the frame are preserved for further processing.

3.3 Evaluation

To fairly evaluate the pixel processing capabilities of different methods, we need to compare only the pixel processing components. As a result, in this part, we focus on the PPU and AM of HARP [6], the Saliency Model of HMAX [12], and our pixel processor design. All these components are designed to do Temporal Saliency and Spatial Saliency comparison.

Table 2. Performance Evaluation

Architecture	Slice LUT	FF	BRAM	Power
PPU + AM (HARP) [6]	154404	2107744	27	2.044
Saliency Model (HMAX) [12]	62440	-	159	13
Our Pixel Processor	8411	12493	19	2.049

Table 2 compares the performance of different pixel processing units. In terms of Slice LUT usage, the combination of the PPU and the AM in HARP [6] uses 154,404 LUTs, indicating a higher resource occupancy rate and greater logic complexity, occupying about 13% of the available resources. In contrast, the Saliency Model combined with HMAX [12] uses only 62,440 Slice LUTs. Our design achieves significantly lower Slice LUT usage, requiring only 8,411 LUTs, demonstrating that our logic is more concise and resource-efficient, utilizing the least amount of resources among the compared designs, representing a 94.55% reduction in LUT usage compared to HARP [6].

For FFs, PPU + AM (HARP [6]) utilizes 2,107,744 FFs, occupying a significant portion of the available resources in the FPGA. This high resource allocation may impact the availability of other system parts or additional functionalities. Such a high number of FFs can lead to increased power consumption and may require a larger FPGA to accommodate the design, resulting in higher costs. In contrast, our design uses only 12,943 FFs, indicating a more efficient use of FF resources, with a 99.39% reduction compared to HARP [6].

Regarding BRAM usage, PPU + AM (HARP [6]) uses 27 BRAMs, while the Saliency Model combined with HMAX [12] uses 159 BRAMs. Our design uses the least BRAM, at 19. The efficiency of HARP and our design in BRAM usage demonstrates their resource management advantages. Our design, with minimal BRAM usage, achieves resource optimization while maintaining functional integrity. This not only helps to reduce power consumption and costs but also improves the flexibility and adaptability of the design in various application scenarios, representing a 29.63% reduction in BRAM usage compared to HARP.

Regarding power consumption, PPU + AM (HARP [6]) has a power usage of 2.044 W, our design consumes 2.049 W, and the Saliency Model (HMAX [12]) consumes 13 W. The similarity in power consumption between our design and HARP [6] can be attributed to optimized resource usage and efficient parallel processing. Both designs leverage advanced power management techniques and operate within the same FPGA fabric, which includes a consistent baseline power consumption. Despite achieving significant reductions in LUT, FF, and BRAM usage, the overall power consumption remains comparable due to these shared efficiency strategies and inherent static power characteristics of the FPGA.

Overall, as Table 2 shows, our design excels in resource utilization, power consumption, and simplicity of design. This makes it a more economical and efficient option, providing better performance and adaptability, and giving it a competitive advantage in a wide range of application scenarios.

4   Conclusion

This paper presents a comprehensive video processing system based on the Xilinx Zynq-7000 SoC [13] architecture. We propose a dual-channel architecture for image processing that provides filtered pixel data suitable for high-level processing, which is beneficial for applications such as scene recognition and object detection from video data streams. This design demonstrates significant hardware optimization compared to existing designs, such as the previously mentioned HARP [6] and HMAX [12]. We plan to integrate attention-based architectures into our system for future work and propose an optimized memory usage loop structure to accelerate the entire pipeline. These enhancements are expected to improve the near-sensor event camera architecture significantly, enabling more efficient real-time processing and reducing latency in edge applications.

In the future, we are also expecting add hardware security methods in our system,

Acknowledgements. I would like to extend my sincere gratitude to the individuals and organizations whose support has been instrumental in the completion of this work.

First and foremost, I wish to express my deep appreciation to my advisor, Dr. Christophe Bobda, from the Department of Electrical and Computer Engineering at the University of Florida. His unwavering guidance, insightful advice, and continuous support have been invaluable throughout the course of my research.

I am also deeply grateful to my family—Jennifer, Jimmy, and my cute little cousin Albert—for their love and encouragement, which have been a source of strength in both my research and personal life.

Lastly, this publication is based upon works supported by the National Science Foundation under Grant No. 2106610 and 2007210. National Science Foundation has been essential in facilitating my research and enabling the pursuit of my academic goals.

References

1. Bobda, C., Velipasalar, S.: Distributed Embedded Smart Cameras. Springer (2014). https://doi.org/10.1007/978-1-4614-7705-1
2. Anders, J., Mefenza, M., Bobda, C., Yonga, F., Aklah, Z., Gunn, K.: A hardware/software prototyping system for driving assistance investigations. J. Real Time Image Process. **11**(3), 559–569 (2016). https://doi.org/10.1007/S11554-013-0351-4
3. Gallego, G., et al.: Event-based vision: a survey. IEEE Trans. Pattern Anal. Mach. Intell. **44**(1), 154–180 (2020)
4. Cannici, M., Ciccone, M., Romanoni, A., Matteucci, M.: Asynchronous convolutional networks for object detection in neuromorphic cameras. In: Proceedings of the IEEE/CVF Conference on Computer Vision and Pattern Recognition Workshops (CVPRW) (2019)
5. Pantho, M.J.H., Bhowmik, P., Bobda, C.: Towards an efficient CNN inference architecture enabling in-sensor processing. Sensors **21**(6), 1955 (2021)
6. Bhowmik, P., Pantho, M.J.H., Bobda, C.: Harp: hierarchical attention oriented region-based processing for high-performance computation in vision sensor. Sensors **21**(5), 1757 (2021)
7. Hoseini, S., Linares-Barranco, B.: Real-time temporal frequency detection in FPGA using event-based vision sensor. In: 2018 IEEE 14th International Conference on Intelligent Computer Communication and Processing (ICCP), pp. 271–278. IEEE (2018)
8. Lu, X., Mao, X., Liu, H., Meng, X., Rai, L.: Event camera point cloud feature analysis and shadow removal for road traffic sensing. IEEE Sensors J. **22**(4), 3358–3369 (2021)
9. Jiang, C., et al.: Energy aware edge computing: a survey. Comput. Commun. **151**, 556–580 (2020)
10. Gehrig, D., Rebecq, H., Gallego, G., Scaramuzza, D.: Asynchronous, photometric feature tracking using events and frames. In: Proceedings of the European Conference on Computer Vision (ECCV), pp. 750–765 (2018)
11. Kumar, M.P.P., Panda, S.K.: Design and verification of DDR SDRAM memory controller using SystemVerilog for higher coverage. In: 2019 International Conference on Intelligent Computing and Control Systems (ICCS), pp. 689–694 (2019)
12. Park, M. S., Zhang, C., DeBole, M., Kestur, S.: Accelerators for biologically-inspired attention and recognition. In: Proceedings of the 50th Annual Design Automation Conference (DAC) (2013)
13. Xilinx: Zynq-7000 SoC configurable logic block (2016). https://www.xilinx.com/products/silicon-devices/soc/zynq-7000.html. Accessed 4 July 2024

14. Mishra, G., Aung, Y. L., Wu, M., Lam, S. K., Srikanthan, T.: Real-time image resizing hardware accelerator for object detection algorithms. In: Proceedings of the 2013 International Conference on Image Processing (ICIP) (2013)
15. Yu, B., Wu, J., Islam, M.J.: UDepth: fast monocular depth estimation for visually-guided underwater robots. arXiv preprint arXiv:2209.12358 (2023)
16. Zhang, X., Eltouny, K., Liang, X., Behdad, S.: Automatic screw detection and tool recommendation system for robotic disassembly. J. Manuf. Sci. Eng. **145**(3), 031008 (2023)
17. Nerella, S., et al.: Transformers and large language models in healthcare: a review. Artif. Intell. Med. **154**, 102900 (2024). https://doi.org/10.1016/j.artmed.2024.102900
18. Albizu, A., et al.: Machine-learning defined precision tDCS for improving cognitive function. Brain Stimulation **16**(3), 969–974 (2023). https://doi.org/10.1016/j.brs.2023.05.020

Hardware-Aware Deep Learning for Edge and Mobile Platforms

Comparing Quantization Techniques for DNNs in Precision Agriculture

Domenic Drechsel, Ali Ehteshami Bejnordi[(⊠)], Stefan Henkler,
and Kristian Rother

Hochschule Hamm-Lippstadt, Hamm, Germany
{domenic.drechsel,ali.ehteshami-bejnordi,stefan.henkler,
kristian.rother}@hshl.de

Abstract. Quantization of deep neural networks has emerged as an enabler for deploying these models on resource-constrained edge devices. This paper evaluates current quantization techniques using a custom dataset for agricultural applications, specifically for detecting sugarbeet plants and weeds from an aerial perspective. The experimental results demonstrate significant improvements in inference speed with minimal accuracy loss whilst achieving state-of-the-art compression rates for both ResNet18 and ResNet50 architectures.

1 Introduction

The advancement of deep neural networks (DNNs) has significantly impacted various areas such as computer vision, speech recognition, and natural language processing [4,7,11]. The deployment of these models on resource-constrained devices remains a challenge due to their large size and computational complexity. Quantization has emerged as a promising technique to address these issues. This is done by reducing the precision of network weights and activations, thereby compressing the model and speeding up inference with a possible drop in accuracy [3,6,17].

In the agricultural domain, precision farming techniques based on DNN are increasingly being adopted to enhance productivity and sustainability [1,2,9]. One critical application is the detection and automated removal of weeds, which can significantly reduce the use of chemical herbicides and promote environmentally friendly farming practices. As shown in [1,2], a network based solution for example with 5G might be possible but is problematic as mostly in the relevant rural area a fast network connection to a GPU-server executing the DNN is not supported. Edge solutions are therefore an enabler for these scenarios. However, the resource constraints of the end devices, such as drones, must be taken into account.

Therefore, the objective of this study is to investigate the performance of quantized versions of ResNet18 and ResNet50 models on CPU based platforms using a custom dataset from the agricultural domain. In order to achieve this,

© IFIP International Federation for Information Processing 2026
Published by Springer Nature Switzerland AG 2026
M. A. Wehrmeister et al. (Eds.): IESS 2024, IFIP AICT 760, pp. 39–49, 2026.
https://doi.org/10.1007/978-3-032-07102-6_4

most used quantization strategies, including static quantization, dynamic quantization, and Quantization-Aware Training (QAT), are evaluated for their impact on accuracy, inference time, and model size. We mainly focus on Resnet models, as according to [2] these have shown the best results for the application domain under consideration. For this purpose, we have created and used our own data set using drone images.

The remainder of this paper is structured as follows: Sect. 2 provides an overview of related work, Sect. 3 outlines the experiment approach, Sect. 4 presents the results of our experiments and Sect. 5 concludes the paper and provides an outlook for future research.

2   Related Work

Quantization has been extensively studied as a method to reduce the computational complexity and memory footprint of DNNs. Early works focused on reducing the precision of weights to accomplish the goals. Courbariaux introduced BinaryConnect, which constrains weights to +1 and -1 during training, significantly reducing memory usage and computation requirements [3]. This approach laid the groundwork for subsequent methods aiming at low-precision training.

Quantized Neural Networks (QNNs) advanced the field by quantizing both weights and activations. Hubara demonstrated that DNNs could be trained with 8-bit, 4-bit, and even 2-bit precision without significant loss in accuracy [8]. This study highlighted the potential of quantization in maintaining high accuracy while reducing model size.

Han proposed Deep Compression, a comprehensive framework that combines pruning, quantization, and Huffman coding to achieve state-of-the-art compression rates [6]. Their work showed that significant reductions in model size and computational requirements could be achieved without compromising accuracy. This multi-stage approach is particularly relevant for applications requiring both storage efficiency and computational speed.

Recent research has focused on adaptive quantization techniques. Khoram and Li proposed an adaptive method that assigns different bit-widths to weights based on their contribution to the overall loss, achieving significant model size reductions with minimal impact on accuracy [12]. This approach allows for more efficient use of precision, balancing the trade-off between model size and performance.

Quantization-Aware Training (QAT) seems to be a powerful technique to mitigate accuracy loss during quantization by simulating the process during training, allowing models to adapt to lower precision. Jacob showed that QAT could achieve near full-precision accuracy with highly quantized models, making it a practical solution for deploying DNNs on resource-constrained devices [10].

Surveys by Gholami and others have compared different quantization methods, highlighting the trade-offs between static and dynamic quantization [5].

These studies provide a comprehensive overview of the advantages and limitations of various techniques, guiding the selection of appropriate methods for specific applications.

In the context of agriculture, precision farming techniques leveraging DNNs have shown promise in improving crop management and reducing environmental impact. Studies by Milioto and Sa have demonstrated the use of DNNs for crop and weed segmentation in aerial imagery, emphasizing the need for efficient models that can be deployed on edge devices for real-time applications [13, 16].

Overall, the quantization work provides a solid foundation for our study, which aims to apply these techniques to a custom dataset of sugar beet and weed images to detect weeds in real-time from the air using drones.

3 Experiments

This section provides an overview of the experimental setup. The experiments were designed to evaluate the impact of various quantization techniques on the performance of two popular deep neural network architectures, ResNet18 and ResNet50, using a custom dataset of sugarbeet and weed images captured by a drone. The dataset includes 3,166 images of sugarbeet and 262 images of weeds. The objective was to assess the trade-offs between accuracy, inference time, and model size for each quantization method.

Subsection 3.1 describes the dataset, Subsect. 3.2 describes the augmentation techniques that were used, Subsect. 3.3 describes the general setup of the experiment, Subsect. 3.4 outlines the used quantization approaches and Subsect. 3.5 gives an overview of the used evaluation metrics.

3.1 Overview of the Dataset

The custom dataset used in this study consists of aerial images from a sugar beat field in the German city of Erftstadt. A drone was used to captured videos of the field at approximately two meters of hight. Images were extracted from the video frames with a custom Python script. This was done by processing the images and converting them to HSV color space using OpenCV. Then, a color threshold was applied to create a binary mask of plant areas. After that, connected component analysis was applied on the binary mask to identify contiguous areas of plants and crop distinct regions that meet minimum size, saving them to an output directory. Finally, the foundation model CLIP [15] was used to classify these extracted patches into weeds and sugar beets. Example images of some of these sugar beets and weeds are shown in Figs. 1 and 2 respectively.

3.2 Data Augmentation

Data augmentation techniques were applied to increase the diversity of the training data and improve the robustness of the models. The following augmentations were used:

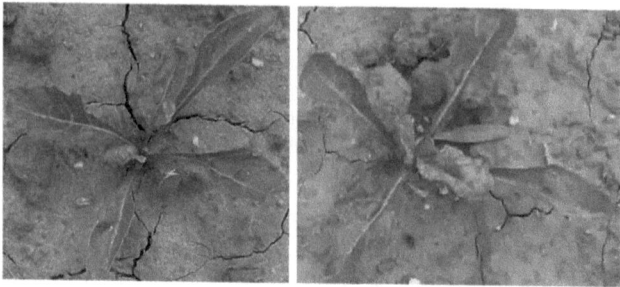

Fig. 1. Example images of sugarbeet from the dataset.

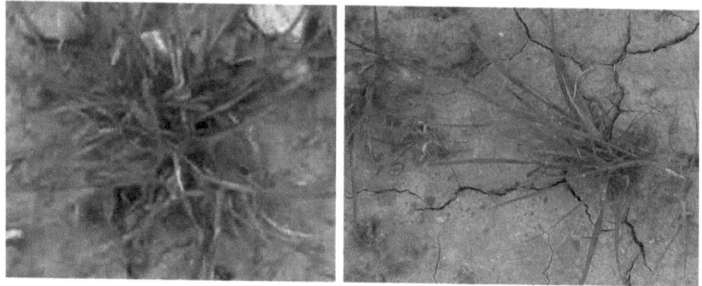

Fig. 2. Example images of weeds from the dataset.

- **Random Rotation**: Images were rotated by a random angle within a specified range.
- **Horizontal and Vertical Flipping**: Images were flipped horizontally and vertically with a probability of 0.5.
- **Random Cropping**: Random crops were taken from the images to simulate different perspectives.
- **Color Jittering**: Brightness, contrast, and saturation of the images were randomly adjusted.

These augmentations help the models generalize better by providing varied training examples. Figure 3 illustrates the jittering augmentation on a sample image from the dataset with the original image on the left and the augmented image on the right.

3.3 Experimental Setup

The dataset was split into training, validation, and test sets using a 70:15:15 ratio, as recommended by [16]. This split ensures that the models are trained on a substantial portion of the data while retaining enough samples for validation and testing to evaluate model performance accurately.

The experiments employed two convolutional neural network architectures: ResNet18 and ResNet50. The experiments were conducted on two hardware platforms: CUDA (GPU) and a multi-core CPU environment. CUDA was employed

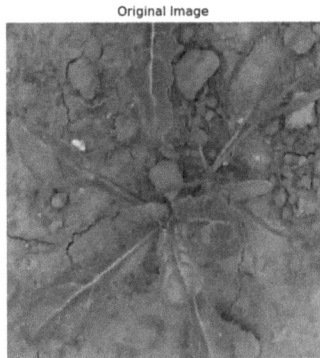
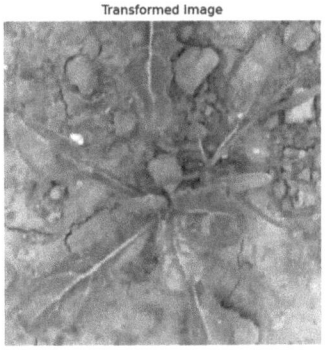

Fig. 3. Example images after data augmentation.

to leverage the parallel processing capabilities of GPUs, while the CPU environment was utilized to evaluate performance on general-purpose processors.

Three quantization techniques were evaluated: dynamic quantization, static quantization, and QAT. Dynamic quantization applies quantization at runtime, converting weights and activations to lower precision on-the-fly. Static quantization is performed post-training, converting weights and potentially activations to lower precision, often 8-bit integers or less. QAT incorporates the quantization process during training, allowing the model to adjust to the lower precision weights and activations.

All models except the QAT model were initially trained using standard full-precision (32-bit) floating-point arithmetic. The training procedure involved the use of a cross-entropy loss function and the SGD optimizer with a learning rate of 0.001. The batch size was 16 and all models were trained for 100 epochs with early stopping.

The ResNet18 and ResNet50 models were pre-trained on the ImageNet dataset and subsequently fine-tuned on our custom dataset. The cross-entropy loss function and the SGD optimizer with a learning rate of 0.001 were employed. Each model was trained for 100 epochs, and early stopping was implemented to prevent overfitting. This approach facilitated faster convergence while maintaining high accuracy; however, further experiments involving other datasets or training techniques could enhance generalization.

3.4 Quantization Methods

The ResNet18 and ResNet50 models were subjected to 8-bit dynamic quantization, static quantization and QAT using the Brevitas library [14].

The dynamic quantization approach offers the advantage of being straightforward to implement without requiring retraining of the model. This method might introduce some quantization noise during inference, potentially affecting the model's accuracy.

Static quantization was conducted subsequent to training on both models. This technique converts the weights and activations to 8-bit integers following the completion of the training process in full precision. Static quantization typically achieves great compression ratios in comparison to dynamic quantization, as it markedly reduces the model size. However, it also may introduce quantization noise that affects the model's accuracy. The advantage of static quantization is its capacity to significantly reduce the model size without necessitating alterations to the training process. By removing 24 of the 32 bits, the resulting model's size should be around one quarter of the original size.

QAT was employed during the training phase of the models. QAT simulates the quantization process during training, enabling the model to adapt to lower precision weights and activations. This technique frequently yields the highest accuracy among quantization methods, as it minimizes the impact of the quantization noise. However, QAT needs greater computational resources during training making it a more resource-intensive process compared to post-training quantization methods.

3.5   Evaluation Metrics

The accuracy of the quantized models was evaluated on a held-out test set from the custom dataset. The inference time was quantified by averaging the time required to process one image. The model size was recorded as the size of the saved model file on disk. The performance of the quantized models was evaluated based on the following metrics:

– **Accuracy**: The classification accuracy of the models on the test set. This is represented as the average from 100 inferences.
– **Inference Time**: The average time taken to process one image during inference. This is also represented as the average time from 100 inferences.
– **Model Size**: The size of the saved model file on disk.

4   Results

In this section, we show our results for the different quantization techniques (dynamic, static and QAT) that were applied to ResNet18 and ResNet50 and discuss their influence on accuracy, inference time and size on disk.

Subsection 4.1 summarizes the results for the ResNet18 architecture, Subsect. 4.2 summarizes the results for the ResNet50 architecture, Subsect. 4.3 gives an overview of the accuracy, Subsect. 4.4 gives an overview of the inference times and Subsect. 4.5 gives an overview of the model sizes.

4.1   ResNet18

Table 1 presents the accuracy, inference time, and model size for ResNet18 under different quantization schemes (dynamic, static and QAT) and for the non-quantized CUDA and CPU platforms.

Table 1. Quantization Results for ResNet18.

Quantization	Platform	Accuracy (%)	Inference Time (ms)	Size (MB)
None	CUDA	90.1	7.74	46.84
None	CPU	90.1	15.76	46.84
Dynamic	CPU	89.5	16.82	45.30
Static	CPU	89.7	9.23	11.93
QAT	CPU	89.3	7.99	11.93

Without quantization, the accuracy was 90.1% for both the CUDA and CPU platform. The average inference time was 7.74 and 15.76 milliseconds (ms) per image on these platforms with a size on disk of 46.84 megabytes (MB). After dynamic quantization, the accuracy dropped to 89.5% while the inference time increased to 16.82 ms and the disk space was slightly decreased to 45.30 MB. After static quantization, the accuracy dropped to 89.7% while the inference time was 9.23 ms and the disk size decreased to 11.93 MB. For QAT, the accuracy was 89.3%, the inference time was 7.99 ms and the space on disk was also 11.93 MB.

4.2   ResNet50

Table 2 presents the accuracy, inference time, and model size for the ResNet50 architecture under different quantization schemes (dynamic, static and QAT) and for the non-quantized CUDA and CPU platforms.

Table 2. Quantization Results for ResNet50.

Quantization	Platform	Accuracy (%)	Inference Time (ms)	Size (MB)
None	CUDA	94.5	6.06	102.55
None	CPU	94.5	53.33	102.55
Dynamic	CPU	93.9	57.17	96.40
Static	CPU	94.3	18.84	26.58
QAT	CPU	93.6	19.04	26.58

Without quantization, the accuracy was 94.5% for both the CUDA and CPU platform. The average inference time was 6.06 and 53.33 ms per image on these platforms with a size on disk of 102.55 MB. After dynamic quantization, the accuracy dropped to 93.9% while the inference time increased to 57.17 ms and the disk space was slightly decreased to 96.40 MB. After static quantization, the accuracy dropped to 94.3% while the inference time was 18.84 ms and the disk size decreased to 26.5. For QAT, the accuracy was 93.6%, the inference time was 19.04 ms and the space on disk was also 26.58 MB.

4.3   Accuracy

For ResNet18, dynamic quantization resulted in a loss of 0.67% of accuracy while static quantization resulted in a loss of 0.44% of accuracy and QAT resulted in a loss of 0.89% of accuracy.

For ResNet50, dynamic quantization resulted in a loss of 0.63% of accuracy while static quantization resulted in a loss of 0.21% of accuracy and QAT resulted in a loss of 0.95% of accuracy.

Overall, the change in accuracy due to quantization was minimal for both ResNet18 and ResNet50 for all quantization methods (<1%). Static quantization preserved the accuracy the best for both architectures while QAT yielded the highest accuracy loss with dynamic quantization in the middle. These results align with the findings of Courbariaux [3] and Han [6].

4.4   Inference Time

The results demonstrate that quantization techniques can improve inference time on the CPU. The full-precision ResNet18 model has an inference time per image of 15.76 ms on the CPU. Dynamic quantization increased the inference time to 16.82 ms. However, static quantization resulted in a notable reduction in inference time, with a value of 9.23 ms (58.57% of the time needed on the CPU). Furthermore, QAT demonstrated an additional improvement in inference time, reaching a value of 7.99 ms (50.70% of the time needed on the CPU), establishing it as the fastest among the tested quantization techniques on the CPU. For comparison, the inference time on CUDA was 7.74 ms.

Similarly, for ResNet50, the full-precision model exhibited an inference time of 53.33 ms on the CPU and 6.06 ms on CUDA. Dynamic quantization also resulted in a slightly higher inference time, raising the inference time to 57.17 ms on the CPU. Static quantization, however, led to a reduction in inference time, with a value of 18.84 ms on the CPU (35.33% of the time needed on the CPU). The QAT achieved a nearly similar inference time of 19.04 ms (35.70% of the time needed on the CPU), thereby demonstrating the effectiveness of both techniques in improving inference speed.

These improvements in inference time are consistent with the results reported by Jacob [10], who showed that QAT could achieve efficient inference speeds with minimal accuracy loss. Hubara [8] also reported significant speed-ups using low-precision weights, supporting the feasibility of these techniques for our use-case.

4.5   Model Size

For ResNet18, the dynamically quantized model used 97.87% of disk space compared to the original model while static quantization and QAT used only 25.47%. Similarly, for ResNet50, the dynamically quantized model used 94.00% of disk space compared to the original model while static quantization and QAT used only 25.92%. Our static quantization results confirm the effectiveness of these approaches in practical settings on a domain specific dataset. These results align with the compression rates reported by Han [6] in their Deep Compression framework. The significant reduction in model size observed in our experiments confirms the effectiveness of static quantization and QAT in practical deployment scenarios.

5 Conclusion and Outlook

In this study, we explored the application of dynamic quantization, static quantization and QAT for ResNet18 and ResNet50 models for detecting sugarbeet plants and weeds from aerial imagery.

Overall, the experimental results indicate that static quantization and QAT result in notable reductions in model size and inference time while maintaining high accuracy. In contrast, dynamic quantization, despite being more straightforward to implement, yielded less favorable results in terms of accuracy and model size reduction.

The findings indicate that quantization techniques, particularly static quantization and QAT, can be effectively utilized in precision agriculture, facilitating the deployment of deep learning models on resource-constrained devices for real-time weed detection. Nevertheless, while our results align with those of public datasets in terms of model size and accuracy trade-offs, more detailed comparisons with similar domain-specific datasets would further substantiate the efficacy of these techniques in agricultural applications. Furthermore, an investigation into sub-8-bit and mixed-precision quantization, particularly for FPGA deployment, could potentially result in even higher compression ratios and inference speeds. It would also be beneficial for future studies to assess whether these findings can be extended beyond the detection of sugarbeet and weeds to other crop types or image modalities, such as multispectral or satellite imagery.

The results of our study on quantizing ResNet18 and ResNet50 are in accordance with the findings reported in public datasets, indicating a reduction in model size and minimal loss of accuracy. Specifically, static quantization on our dataset resulted in a 3.92x reduction in model size with less than 1% accuracy degradation, which is comparable to the findings of Han et al. [8]. The results of Quantization-Aware Training (QAT) also matched those from Jacob et al. [10], maintaining accuracy within 1% of the baseline. However, direct comparisons with domain-specific datasets, particularly in agriculture, are lacking, which would provide a more comprehensive understanding of how these methods perform in similar contexts.

Future research could explore the integration of these quantization techniques with other model compression methods, such as pruning and knowledge distillation, to further enhance the performance of neural networks. Additionally, extending the study to include other crops, weed species and models could provide broader insights into the generalizability of these techniques. Lastly, quantized models are a good starting point for inference on FPGAs which could be an interesting approach in resource constrained domains.

Acknowledgment. This research is supported by the Ministry of Economic Affairs, Industry, Climate Action and Energy of the State of North Rhine-Westphalia. Cofunded by the European Union. Grant number EFRE-20800498.

References

1. Alao, O.B., Rother, K., Henkler, S.: Synthetic data for machine learning on embedded systems in precision agriculture. In: Henkler, S., Kreutz, M., Wehrmeister, M.A., Götz, M., Rettberg, A. (eds.) Designing Modern Embedded Systems: Software, Hardware, and Applications, pp. 127–138. Springer Nature Switzerland, Cham (2023). https://doi.org/10.1007/978-3-031-34214-1_11
2. Brodo, L., Henkler, S., Rother, K.: Analysing the characteristics of neural networks for the recognition of sugar beets. In: Henkler, S., Kreutz, M., Wehrmeister, M.A., Götz, M., Rettberg, A. (eds.) Designing Modern Embedded Systems: Software, Hardware, and Applications, pp. 115–126. Springer Nature Switzerland, Cham (2023). https://doi.org/10.1007/978-3-031-34214-1_10
3. Courbariaux, M., Bengio, Y., David, J.P.: Binaryconnect: training deep neural networks with binary weights during propagations. In: Advances in Neural Information Processing Systems, vol. 28 (2015)
4. Devlin, J., Zbib, R., Huang, Z., Lamar, T., Schwartz, R., Makhoul, J.: Fast and robust neural network joint models for statistical machine translation. In: proceedings of the 52nd Annual Meeting of the Association for Computational Linguistics (Volume 1: Long Papers), pp. 1370–1380 (2014)
5. Gholami, A., Kim, S., Dong, Z., Yao, Z., Mahoney, M.W., Keutzer, K.: A survey of quantization methods for efficient neural network inference. In: Low-Power Computer Vision, pp. 291–326. Chapman and Hall/CRC (2022)
6. Han, S., Mao, H., Dally, W.J.: Deep compression: compressing deep neural networks with pruning, trained quantization and huffman coding. arXiv preprint arXiv:1510.00149 (2015)
7. Hinton, G., et al.: Deep neural networks for acoustic modeling in speech recognition: the shared views of four research groups. IEEE Signal Process. Mag. **29**(6), 82–97 (2012)
8. Hubara, I., Courbariaux, M., Soudry, D., El-Yaniv, R., Bengio, Y.: Quantized neural networks: training neural networks with low precision weights and activations. J. Mach. Learn. Res. **18**(187), 1–30 (2018)
9. Islam, N., Rashid, M.M., Pasandideh, F., Ray, B., Moore, S., Kadel, R.: A review of applications and communication technologies for internet of things (IoT) and unmanned aerial vehicle (UAV) based sustainable smart farming. Sustainability **13**, 1821 (2021)
10. Jacob, B., et al.: Quantization and training of neural networks for efficient integer-arithmetic-only inference. In: Proceedings of the IEEE Conference on Computer Vision and Pattern Recognition, pp. 2704–2713 (2018)
11. Karen, S.: Very deep convolutional networks for large-scale image recognition. arXiv preprint arXiv: 1409.1556 (2014)
12. Khoram, S., Li, J.: Adaptive quantization of neural networks. In: International Conference on Learning Representations (2018)
13. Milioto, A., Lottes, P., Stachniss, C.: Real-time semantic segmentation of crop and weed for precision agriculture robots leveraging background knowledge in CNNs. In: 2018 IEEE International Conference on Robotics and Automation (ICRA), pp. 2229–2235. IEEE (2018)

14. Pappalardo, A.: Xilinx/brevitas (2023). https://doi.org/10.5281/zenodo.3333552
15. Radford, A., et al.: Learning transferable visual models from natural language supervision. In: International Conference on Machine Learning, pp. 8748–8763. PMLR (2021)
16. Sa, I., et al.: Weedmap: a large-scale semantic weed mapping framework using aerial multispectral imaging and deep neural network for precision farming. Remote Sensing $10(9)$, 1423 (2018)
17. Zhao, T., et al.: A survey of deep learning on mobile devices: applications, optimizations, challenges, and research opportunities. Proc. IEEE $110(3)$, 334–354 (2022)

Hardware Acceleration of CNNs with the FINN Framework

Domenic Drechsel, Stefan Henkler$^{(\boxtimes)}$, Sheikh Muhammad Adib Bin Sh Abu Bakar, Kathleen Strodick, Lukas Walter, Kristian Rother, and Ali Ehteshami Bejnordi

Hochschule Hamm-Lippstadt, Hamm, Germany
{domenic.drechsel,stefan.henkler,sheikh.adib,kathleen.strodick,
lukas.walter,kristian.rother,ali.ehteshami-bejnordi}@hshl.de

Abstract. This paper explores the use of Field-Programmable Gate Arrays (FPGAs) to accelerate a Convolutional Neural Network (CNN) for precision agriculture applications using the FINN framework by Xilinx. Our research provides an end-to-end use case from training and quantizing a CNN to running inference on an FPGA. We evaluate the quantized CNN model on a custom dataset for sugar beet and weed classification. The results demonstrate inference-performance improvements, making this FPGA-based implementation a candidate for real-time agricultural monitoring and decision-making.

1 Introduction

Among the neural network architectures, Convolutional Neural Networks (CNNs) have gained prominence due to their exceptional performance in image-related tasks. However, the deployment of these models in resource-constrained environments such as edge devices poses significant challenges. Field-Programmable Gate Arrays (FPGAs) represent a promising solution, offering a customizable hardware platform that can achieve high performance with low power consumption [13].

However, there are few end-to-end use cases that show how to get from training a CNN to running inference on an FPGA, especially in the agricultural domain. That is why this paper explores the use of FPGAs to accelerate a CNN for precision agriculture applications using the FINN framework by Xilinx [9]. The FINN platform enables the deployment of neural networks with a not exclusive focus on Binary Neuronal Networks(BNNs) on FPGAs while maintaining a balance between computational efficiency and model accuracy. Our research is centered on providing an end-to-end use case and evaluating the quantized CNN model on a custom image classification dataset for sugar beets and weeds.

The reason behind utilizing FPGAs for neural network inference is their ability to provide parallel processing capabilities, which reduces inference time in comparison to traditional Central Processing Unit (CPU) and Graphics Processing Unit (GPU) implementations [3]. Moreover, FPGAs offer a flexible architecture that can be tailored to specific application requirements, rendering them suitable for real-time processing in edge computing scenarios [8].

Published by Springer Nature Switzerland AG 2026
M. A. Wehrmeister et al. (Eds.): IESS 2024, IFIP AICT 760, pp. 50–60, 2026.
https://doi.org/10.1007/978-3-032-07102-6_5

The objective of this study is to examine and evaluate the trade-offs inherent to FPGA-based CNN implementations in comparison to their GPU counterparts. In particular, the focus is on performance metrics such as accuracy, inference time, resource utilization, and the impact of quantization techniques. The models are evaluated in terms of their accuracy, inference time and resource utilization. Furthermore, the trade-offs involved are discussed. We also provide a comprehensive technical background to the FINN framework and the specific methodologies employed in our implementations thus providing an end-to-end use case from training and quantizing a CNN to running inference on an FPGA.

The custom dataset utilized in this study comprises aerial images of sugar beet plants and associated weeds. The dataset comprises 22,000 images in two classes: sugar beets (around 7.500 images) and weeds (around 14.500 images). We employed a 80:20 split between the training and testing sets. All images were resized to 256×256 pixels, and data augmentation techniques such as rotation $(+-15°)$, flipping, and random cropping were applied to increase the dataset's diversity. These preprocessing steps are designed to provide a more robust training experience for the model, thereby facilitating better generalization in real-world scenarios.

The paper is structured as follows: Sect. 2 presents a review of related work on neural network acceleration using FPGAs and other platforms. Section 3 presents an analysis of FPGAs for CNN acceleration. In Sect. 4 we present features and advantages of the FINN framework. Section 5 details the design and development process of our FPGA-based models. This is followed by the presentation of the results of our experiments in Sect. 6, comparing the performance of different models. Finally, we conclude with a summary of our findings and future research directions in Sect. 7.

2   Related Work

The use of FPGAs for accelerating neural network inference has been extensively explored in recent years. Zhang et al. [13] presented an FPGA-based accelerator design for deep CNNs, demonstrating significant performance improvements over traditional CPU and GPU implementations. Their work laid the groundwork for subsequent research in this area by highlighting the potential of FPGAs to provide high computational efficiency and low latency.

Farabet et al. [3] introduced NeuFlow, a runtime reconfigurable dataflow processor designed for vision applications. NeuFlow leverages the parallelism and reconfigurability of FPGAs to achieve high performance in real-time image processing tasks. This work emphasized the importance of hardware-software co-design in maximizing the efficiency of FPGA-based accelerators.

Shawahna et al. [8] reviewed various FPGA-based accelerators for deep learning networks, focusing on the trade-offs between performance, power consumption, and resource utilization. Their comprehensive survey underscored the versatility of FPGAs in adapting to different neural network architectures and application requirements.

The development of frameworks like FINN [9] and HLS4ML [1] has further facilitated the deployment of neural networks on FPGAs. FINN, in particular, targets BNNs and provides a scalable solution for mapping these networks to FPGA hardware. Umuroglu et al. [9] demonstrated the effectiveness of FINN in achieving low-latency, high-throughput inference for various image classification tasks.

Other works include Qiu et al. [7], who explored the deployment of CNNs on embedded FPGA platforms. Their research highlighted the potential of FPGAs to deliver high performance in power-constrained environments. Venieris and Bouganis [10] developed FPGAConvNet, a framework for mapping CNNs onto FPGAs, emphasizing the importance of optimizing both the neural network architecture and the FPGA resources for maximum efficiency.

Despite these advancements, several challenges remain in optimizing neural network inference on FPGAs. Issues such as model quantization, resource management, and latency reduction continue to be areas of active research. Our work builds on these foundations by evaluating the performance of CNN models with different bit-widths on FPGAs, using the FINN framework to achieve efficient hardware implementations.

3   FPGAs for CNN Acceleration

The deployment of CNNs on FPGAs has gained significant traction due to the demand for efficient, low-latency inference in edge computing and real-time applications. The inherent parallelism and reconfigurability of FPGAs make them ideal candidates for accelerating CNN inference. However, several challenges must be addressed to optimize the performance and efficiency of these implementations. In Subsect. 3.1 we provide a basic overview of FPGAs. In Subsect. 3.2 we outline how neural network acceleration on FPGAs works. In Subsect. 3.3 we outline the challenges with CNNs on FPGAs and in Subsect. ?? we provide an overview of state-of-the-art FPGA frameworks.

3.1   FPGAs

FPGAs are integrated circuits that can be configured by the user after manufacturing. They consist of an array of programmable logic blocks and a hierarchy of reconfigurable interconnects, which allows designers to implement custom hardware functionalities [2]. FPGAs offer a number of advantages over traditional hardware acceleration methods, including flexibility, parallelism, and low latency. As a result, they are an optimal choice for the deployment of deep learning models in edge computing environments.

The architecture of a FPGA consists of logic elements such as Look-Up Tables (LUTs), flip-flops, and Digital Signal Processing (DSP) blocks. These components can be programmed to perform specific tasks, thereby enabling the implementation of complex algorithms directly in hardware [6]. FPGAs also facilitate the use of High-Level Synthesis (HLS) tools, which enable designers to describe the functionality of the hardware in question using high-level programming languages such as C/C++.

3.2 Neural Network Acceleration on FPGAs

The acceleration of neural networks on FPGAs necessitates the mapping of the computational graph of a neural network to the hardware resources available on the FPGA. This process requires the optimization of the model to fit within the FPGA's resource constraints while maintaining high throughput and low latency. Several techniques are employed to achieve this, including model quantization, pruning and pipelining [10].

Quantization reduces the precision of the weights and activations, which can significantly reduce the resource requirements and increase the speed of computation [4]. Pruning removes redundant connections in the neural network, further reducing the complexity of the model [5]. Pipelining allows for overlapping of operations, ensuring that the hardware resources are utilized efficiently [14].

3.3 Challenges in FPGA-Based CNN Deployment

3.3.1 Challenges in Deploying CNNs on FPGAs

Deploying CNNs on FPGAs is challenging due to limited hardware resources like LUTs, flip-flops, and DSP blocks. Efficient resource utilization requires optimization techniques such as quantization and pruning [10]. Quantization reduces the precision of weights and activations, minimizing computational and memory demands, though it risks accuracy loss, especially with very low bit-widths [4]. Pruning simplifies networks by removing connections, decreasing resource usage while maintaining performance.

Efficient memory management and dataflow optimization are also critical. CNN inference demands substantial data movement across layers, which can bottleneck performance. Techniques like pipelining and tiling help overlap computations and data transfers, improving throughput and reducing latency [14].

4 The FINN Framework

The FINN framework is specifically designed for the deployment of neural networks on FPGAs [9]. FINN capitalizes on the inherent parallelism of FPGAs to accelerate the inference, thereby providing high throughput and low power consumption.

The framework supports a range of neural network layers and operations, including convolutional, fully connected, and activation layers. Additionally, FINN is compatible with HLS tools, enabling the automated generation of FPGA configurations based on high-level model descriptions [9]. Overall, the benefits of FINN can be summarized as follows:

- **Efficiency**: By using binary values for weights and activations, FINN significantly reduces the computational and memory requirements of neural network models. This leads to faster inference times and lower power consumption [9].
- **Flexibility**: FINN supports a wide range of neural network layers and architectures, allowing users to deploy custom models on FPGAs. The framework also integrates with high-level synthesis tools, enabling easy generation of FPGA configurations from high-level model descriptions [11].
- **Scalability**: FINN's architecture is designed to scale with the available FPGA resources, ensuring optimal utilization of the hardware. This makes it suitable for deploying models of varying complexity on different FPGA platforms.
- **Open-Source**: As an open-source framework, FINN encourages collaboration and innovation in the field of FPGA-based neural network acceleration. Users can contribute to the development of the framework and leverage community support for their projects [9].

The process of getting a CNN to run on an FPGA with FINN is divided into several phases, each of which involves specific tasks and conversions. The following sections describe each phase in detail, following the flowchart depicted in Fig. 1.

- **QNN Training and Export**: In this stage, the Quantized Neural Network (QNN) is trained using frameworks like PyTorch or TensorFlow. Once trained, the network is exported to the FINN-ONNX format, which is a specialized format for handling QNNs in the FINN workflow.
- **Network Preparation and Model Transformation**: After exporting, the network undergoes preparation and model transformation in the following steps:
  - **Streamlining Transformations**: The idea of streamlining is to eliminate floating point operations in a model by moving, summarising and converting them into multi-threshold nodes.
  - **Converting to HLS Layers**: In this step, standard or custom layers are converted to High-Level Synthesis (HLS) layers. These layers correspond to functions in FINN libraries, enabling efficient hardware implementation.
  - **Data Flow Partitioning**: The model is partitioned into HLS and non-HLS layers. The HLS layers are further processed in the FINN workflow, while the non-HLS layers remain in the parent graph. This partitioning is important for managing data flow and optimizing performance.
- **Adjust Folding For Max Performance**: This step involves adjusting the accelerators folding factor to maximize performance on the target FPGA. Folding is a technique used to balance resource usage and performance by adjusting the parallelism of the accelerator.
- **Hardware Build**: The hardware build stage is critical for creating the actual FPGA implementation. In this step, the network is transformed into IP blocks or Verilog code, which are then stitched together to create a cohesive design.

This design is further integrated into a Vivado or Vitis project, preparing it for deployment on the FPGA. It involves several sub-steps:

- **Synthesis (F & R)**: The network is synthesized into a format that can be implemented on the FPGA.
- **PYNG Driver**: A driver is generated to facilitate communication between the FPGA and the host system.
- **Run On Hardware**: The final stage involves deploying the generated design onto the FPGA hardware. The QNN can now perform inference tasks with high efficiency and speed.

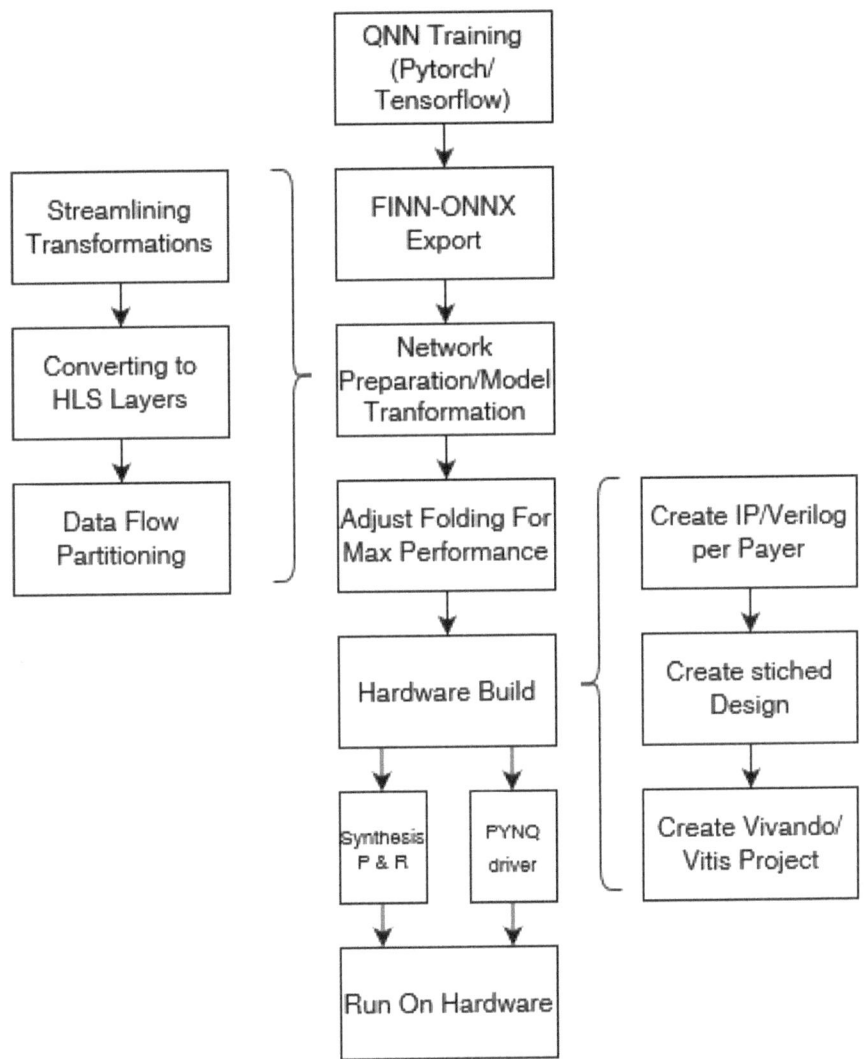

Fig. 1. Flow chart FINN.

5   Implementation

Deploying CNNs on FPGAs via the FINN framework requires a series of complex steps. This section outlines the methodology and techniques used in the implementation process, which includes training, quantization, hardware synthesis, deployment, and validation.

5.1   Data Preparation

The data preparation phase was comprised of several steps. First, the dataset was loaded and subjected to an initial examination to gain an understanding of its structure and content. This entailed examining the distribution of classes, the size of images, and any potential imbalances in the data. During the pre-processing steps the images were resized to a uniform size, pixel values were normalized and the images were converted to a format suitable for training.

Furthermore, data augmentation techniques such as rotation, scaling, flipping, and cropping were employed to enhance the robustness of the trained models by expanding the dataset and facilitate better generalization of the models.

5.2   Model Training and Quantization

The subsequent stage in the implementation process is model training, during which the CNN models were trained on the pre-processed data. The CNN model was quantized using the Brevitas library, which is integrated with the FINN framework for the quantization and export of neural networks to an ONNX format suitable for FPGA deployment. We employed 4-bit quantization for both weights and activations.

The training process encompassed several steps, including the selection of appropriate model architectures, the configuration of hyperparameters, and the optimization of the models using gradient descent algorithms. The selection of model architectures is guided by the specific requirements of the application, such as the desired trade-off between accuracy and computational complexity. For the purpose of this study, we used a simple CNN as a starting point, as recommended by the FINN documentation.

The CNN utilized in this study comprises six layers: two convolutional layers, followed by max pooling, batch normalization, and two fully connected layers. The final output layer employs the softmax function for classification purposes. A 4-bit quantized model was utilized for deployment on the FPGA. Batch normalization was implemented after each convolutional layer to accelerate convergence during training. Pooling layers were incorporated to downsample the feature maps, and the depth of the network was adjusted to align with the FPGA's resource constraints while maintaining accuracy.

5.3 Hardware Synthesis and Deployment

Hardware synthesis represents the process of transforming the quantized models into hardware descriptions that can be deployed on FPGAs. The FINN framework employs High-Level Synthesis (HLS) tools to generate the hardware descriptions from the quantized models, which are subsequently synthesized and implemented on FPGA devices [9].

The hardware synthesis process encompasses a number of stages, including the generation of Hardware Description Language (HDL) code, the synthesis of the HDL code into gate-level representations, and the placement and routing of the synthesized designs on the FPGA fabric. The HDL tools utilized by the FINN framework facilitate the generation of optimized hardware descriptions that leverage the parallel processing capabilities of FPGAs to achieve high throughput and low latency [1, 10].

In regard to the hardware, the model was deployed on a Alveo U280 FPGA and the results were compared to those obtained from a GPU implementation on an NVIDIA A100. In order to obtain the inference times for the GPU, PyTorch was used with a batch size of 128. In contrast, the troughput and hardware usage for the FPGA were taken from the Vitis/Vivado results.

5.4 Optimization and Validation

The final stage of the implementation process involves the optimization and validation of the deployed models to ensure their performance and efficiency. This stage encompasses several key activities, including the optimization of the hardware designs to minimize resource utilization, the validation of the models on real-world data, and the evaluation of the overall system performance [10].

The optimization techniques employed during this stage include the pruning of redundant connections, the implementation of efficient memory management strategies, and the implementation of pipelining and parallelism to enhance throughput. These techniques are applied iteratively to refine the hardware designs and to achieve the desired balance between performance and resource utilization. [4, 9].

The validation process entails the examination of deployed models on actual data sets. This process offers invaluable insights into the efficacy of the models in practical scenarios, facilitating the identification of potential avenues for further enhancement. The assessment of the overall system performance encompasses metrics such as accuracy, throughput, latency, and resource utilization, which are utilized to benchmark the performance of the deployed models against contemporary benchmarks [12].

In conclusion, the implementation of CNN models on FPGAs using the FINN framework is a comprehensive and iterative process that encompasses model training, quantization, hardware synthesis, deployment, and validation. By employing a variety of optimization techniques and addressing implementation challenges, significant improvements in performance and efficiency have been achieved.

6   Results

Table 1 summarizes the inference time and accuracy for the 4-bit model for the GPU and FPGA platforms.

Table 1. Model Evaluation Metrics on GPU and FPGA

Model	Bit-width	Platform	Inference Time (ms)	Accuracy (%)
CNN	4-bit	GPU	2.4281	75.1
CNN	4-bit	FPGA	0.5102	75.2

The inference time on the FPGA of 0.5102 ms is significantly lower than the inference time of 2.4281 ms on the GPU. Meanwhile, the accuracy is nearly the same with a difference of 0.1%.

The detailed FPGA evaluation includes metrics such as runtime, throughput, DRAM bandwidth, and various input/output times. These metrics provide a deeper understanding of the performance and efficiency of the FPGA implementation. The result is presented in tabular form in Table 2.

Table 2. Detailed FPGA Performance Metrics

Model	Runtime (ms)	Throughput (images/s)	DRAM in (MB/s)	DRAM out (MB/s)	Fclk (MHz)
CNN 4-bit	65.236	1962.11	5.3475	0.0017	100

The metrics in Table 2 highlight the efficiency of the FPGA implementation. The runtime for the 4-bit CNN model at a clock frequency (Fclk) of 100 MHz was 65.236 ms, with a throughput of 1740.74 images per second. The utilization of the dynamic random-access memory (DRAM) bandwidth is minimal at 5.3475 MB/s, indicating the presence of efficient memory access patterns.

The high throughput values demonstrate the FPGA's capacity to process a considerable number of inferences per second, rendering it suitable for real-time applications. The low DRAM bandwidth usage indicates that the data movement between the DRAM and the FPGA is optimized, thereby reducing potential bottlenecks and ensuring smooth data flow.

7   Conclusion

This paper presents an end-to-end use case for the implementation of a CNN model on a FPGA using the FINN framework. By evaluating the resulting 4-bit CNN model on our custom dataset from the agricultural domain, we demonstrated the trade-offs between model accuracy and inference time.

Our findings indicate that 4-bit quantized FPGA implementations can achieve significantly lower inference times compared to their GPU counterparts while not sacrificing much accuracy. This makes them highly suitable for real-time applications in edge computing. Although there is a slight reduction in accuracy, the benefits of reduced latency and power consumption can make this a worthwhile trade.

Future work will focus on exploring further optimizations, different bit-widths and extending the evaluation to other types of neural networks. Additionally, the integration of more advanced quantization techniques and the development of custom FPGA architectures tailored to specific applications will be investigated. Furthermore, the assessment of performance on a bespoke agricultural dataset offers invaluable insights into the operation of these models in real-world scenarios. Despite its modest size, the bespoke dataset enabled us to evaluate the FPGA's capacity to process image classification tasks in a resource-constrained environment.

References

1. Aarrestad, T., Loncar, V., Ghielmetti, N., et al.: Fast convolutional neural networks on FPGAs with hls4ml. arXiv preprint arXiv:2101.05108 (2021)
2. Compton, K., Hauck, S.: Reconfigurable computing: a survey of systems and software. ACM Comput. Surv. (CSUR) **34**(2), 171–210 (2002)
3. Farabet, C., Poulet, C., Han, H., LeCun, Y.: Neuflow: a runtime reconfigurable dataflow processor for vision. In: CVPR 2011 WORKSHOPS, pp. 109–116 (2011)
4. Han, S., Mao, H., Dally, W.J.: Deep compression: compressing deep neural networks with pruning, trained quantization and huffman coding. arXiv preprint arXiv:1510.00149 (2015)
5. Han, S., Pool, J., Tran, J., Dally, W.: Learning both weights and connections for efficient neural network. arXiv preprint arXiv:1506.02626 (2015)
6. Kuon, I., Rose, J.: FPGA architecture: survey and challenges. Found. Trends Electron. Des. Autom. **2**(2), 135–253 (2007)
7. Qiu, J., et al.: Going deeper with embedded FPGA platform for convolutional neural network. In: Proceedings of the 2016 ACM/SIGDA International Symposium on Field-Programmable Gate Arrays, pp. 26–35 (2016)
8. Shawahna, A., Sait, S.M., El-Maleh, A.: FPGA-based accelerators of deep learning networks for learning and classification: a review. IEEE Access **7**, 7823–7859 (2019)
9. Umuroglu, Y., et al.: Finn: a framework for fast, scalable binarized neural network inference. arXiv preprint arXiv:1612.07119 (2017)
10. Venieris, S.I., Bouganis, C.S.: FPGAConvnet: a framework for mapping convolutional neural networks on FPGAs. In: Proceedings of the 2016 ACM/SIGDA International Symposium on Field-Programmable Gate Arrays, pp. 291–296 (2016)
11. Venieris, S.I., Bouganis, C.S.: Toolflows for mapping convolutional neural networks on FPGAs: a survey and future directions. ACM Comput. Surv. (CSUR) **51**(3), 1–39 (2018)
12. Westby, I., Yang, X., Liu, T., Xu, H.: FPGA acceleration on a multi-layer perceptron neural network for digit recognition. J. Supercomputing (2021). https://doi.org/10.1007/s11227-021-03849-7, https://sci-hub.se/10.1007/s11227-021-03849-7

13. Zhang, C., Li, P., Sun, G., Guan, Y., Xiao, B., Cong, J.: Optimizing FPGA-based accelerator design for deep convolutional neural networks. In: Proceedings of the 2015 ACM/SIGDA international symposium on Field-Programmable Gate Arrays, pp. 161–170 (2015)
14. Zhang, C., Sun, G., Xiao, B., Cong, J.: Caffeine: towards uniformed representation and acceleration for deep convolutional neural networks. In: Proceedings of the 35th ACM SIGPLAN Conference on Programming Language Design and Implementation, pp. 1–12 (2016)

Distributed Convolutional Neural Network Training on Mobile and Edge Clusters

Pranav Rama[✉], Madison Threadgill, and Andreas Gerstlauer

Electrical and Computer Engineering, The University of Texas at Austin, Austin, TX, USA
{pranavrama9999,madison.threadgill,gerstl}@utexas.edu

Abstract. The training of deep and/or convolutional neural networks (DNNs/CNNs) is traditionally done on servers with powerful CPUs and GPUs. Recent efforts have emerged to localize machine learning tasks fully on the edge. This brings advantages in reduced latency and increased privacy, but necessitates working with resource-constrained devices. Approaches for inference and training in mobile and edge devices based on pruning, quantization or incremental and transfer learning require trading off accuracy. Several works have explored distributing inference operations on mobile and edge clusters instead. However, there is limited literature on distributed training on the edge. Existing approaches all require a central, potentially powerful edge or cloud server for coordination or offloading. In this paper, we describe an approach for distributed CNN training exclusively on mobile and edge devices. Our approach is beneficial for the initial CNN layers that are feature map dominated. It is based on partitioning forward inference and back-propagation operations among devices through tiling and fusing to maximize locality and expose communication and memory-aware parallelism. We also introduce the concept of layer grouping to further fine-tune performance based on computation and communication trade-off. Results show that for a cluster of 2–6 quad-core Raspberry Pi3 devices, training of an object-detection CNN provides a 2x-15x speedup with respect to a single core and up to 8x reduction in memory usage per device, all without sacrificing accuracy. Grouping offers up to 1.5x speedup depending on the reference profile and batch size.

Keywords: Distributed edge computing · machine learning

1 Introduction

Traditionally, training and inference of deep learning (DL) models is performed in the cloud. This requires a large amount of data to be collected and sent to a centralized infrastructure, introducing latency, privacy, and real-time concerns. Various approaches have proposed to partition the processing between mobile, edge, and cloud resources [1,2]. However, such approaches still rely on a remote cloud for partial processing. To address the latency and privacy concerns when

Published by Springer Nature Switzerland AG 2026
M. A. Wehrmeister et al. (Eds.): IESS 2024, IFIP AICT 760, pp. 61–73, 2026.
https://doi.org/10.1007/978-3-032-07102-6_6

communicating with the cloud, recent efforts have emerged to localize DL tasks fully on mobile or edge devices [3–5]. However, this brings the challenge of performing compute and memory-intensive inference and training operations on such resource-constrained devices.

A wide range of approaches have been proposed to address limited memory and computing capabilities in mobile and edge settings. Techniques such as pruning and quantization focus on decreasing the complexity of the model by removing weights and neurons or reducing the bit precision during inference and/or training. Other approaches such as incremental and transfer learning start from a pre-trained model and only partially update the model to save computational resources and reduce training time. These approaches trade-off accuracy for decreased computational complexity.

Several complementary methods have recently been proposed to utilize parallelism in DL models by partitioning them across multiple devices while preserving the original model and accuracy. Federated learning [6] exploits data parallelism, but still requires a central server for coordination as well as storing and processing of complete models in each device, which is often infeasible given memory constraints. Other approaches partition and distribute the model itself across a cluster of edge devices [5,7–9]. In addition to exploiting available multi-device parallelism, this allows for reducing both the computational and storage requirements on each device. However, such approaches have only been demonstrated for inference so far.

In this paper, we present an approach for distributed CNN training exclusively on communication- and memory-constrained mobile and edge clusters. Our approach targets feature map-dominated early CNN layers. We adopt a tiling and fusing-based partitioning scheme that has previously been demonstrated for inference [7,10,11] and extend it to apply to both forward and back-propagation training tasks. The scheme tiles feature maps to reduce memory footprint and expose model parallelism, then fuses matching tiles of consecutive layers into independent execution stacks placed on each device to maximally exploit locality. Furthermore, groups of layers are formed among tiles where synchronization of feature data shared among neighboring tiles is performed only at group boundaries. At the end of a single training pass, the final weight updates of all stacks are aggregated. This approach can confirm to arbitrary memory constraints imposed by each edge device while exposing parallelism, minimizing communication, and exploiting the locality inherent in convolutional and pooling layers. Our distributed training approach includes the following contributions:

1. We propose a novel method for tiling and fusing of backpropagation tasks that considers memory and communication constraints, while exploiting parallelism for distributed CNN training on resource-constrained device clusters.
2. We apply the concept of layer grouping of forward inference and backpropagation tasks in order to further fine tune computation and communication overhead based on the grouping profile of the layers.
3. We evaluate our approach on distributed training of Yolov2, a common CNN for object detection, distributed across a network of quad-core Rasberry Pis.

2   Related Work

Performing inference on resource-constrained edge and mobile devices has received significant attention. Approaches for distributed inference in edge settings exploit inherent parallelism to partition a model and distribute it across multiple devices [4,5,7–9]. These methods can be applied to the forward inference pass in distributed training. We adopt tiling and fusing strategies from distributed edge and hardware accelerated inference [7,10,11] in our work and extend it to the back-propagation pass in order to support distributed training.

Training CNNs requires additional memory compared to inference due to the need to store input data, gradients, and activation values for each layer. This normally requires partitioning of the workload involving powerful edge servers or the cloud [1,12,13]. Multiple approaches exist for training a DL model on a single edge device [14]. These typically employ simplified model architectures [15] or use reduced bitwidths for training [16]. Alternatively, approaches for incremental or transfer learning take a pre-trained model and only update a subset of weights [17] or the last layers of a model with every training sample [18]. However, all of these approaches trade off accuracy for reduced model complexity.

Multi-device solutions that rely on federated learning exploit data parallelism to collaboratively train a model, with each device training a local model on its own data and devices exchanging weight updates as different variants of a distributed gradient descent [6]. Other multi-device approaches rely on approximate gradient prediction methods that trade off accuracy [19]. However, mobile and edge devices, e.g. in the IoT space, often lack sufficient memory to store an entire local model. In [12,13], federated learning is hierarchically combined with model partitioning in each local cluster. However, these approaches use partitioning schemes commonly used in cloud settings, which are not optimized for the greater memory and communication limitations in mobile and edge settings.

3   Overview

Figure 1 gives an overview of our approach. We partition feature data and delta gradient maps in forward inference and back-propagation passes, respectively, into tiles in a grid-wise fashion along their width and height dimensions. In both passes, output tiles of each layer are computed from input tiles through convolutions with filter data or through simple pooling operations. Exploiting the inherent locality in these operators, all intermediate matching tiles on forward and backward passes are fused into independent execution stacks and tasks that stay local on one device. Tiling exposes parallelism and reduces storage requirements proportional to the tiling granularity, while fusing maximizes locality and thus minimizes communication overhead.

Each output tile is computed by convolving a certain dependent input region with the filter data. This dependent region includes the corresponding input tile along with some boundary data, which depends on the filter size and stride. The boundary data has to be communicated between the neighboring devices prior to starting the convolutions in both the forward and backward passes.

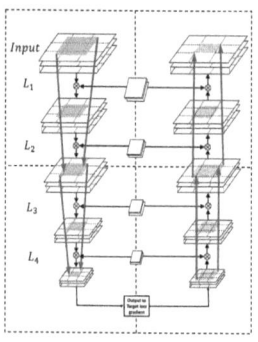
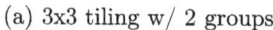

(a) 3x3 tiling w/ 2 groups

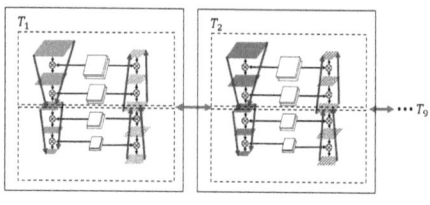

(b) Independent execution tasks with communication boundaries

Fig. 1. Distributed CNN training overview.

Alternatively, we can further combine multiple convolutional and pooling layers to form groups where communication of boundary data with neighboring tiles is done only at the beginning of each group. Within each group, any required intermediate data is locally computed from input data collected at the beginning of the group and no further communication is needed within the group. Figure 1 shows 2 groups each in the forward and backward pass. In this case, communication is done at the feature-map inputs of layer L_1 and L_3 in the forward pass and at the delta gradient inputs of layer L_4 and L_2 in the backward pass. These feature and gradient maps serve as synchronization points where all tiles share boundary data with the neighboring tiles. Grouping introduces a trade off between communication and computation overhead. Larger groups have more redundant computation since the boundary data grows with the group size as illustrated by the funneling red arrows in Fig. 1. At the same time, larger groups synchronize less frequently whereas smaller groups have more communication and synchronization overhead. We will discuss optimal grouping strategies later.

The only points at which the entire partition needs to be communicated is when receiving the input training sample at the first layer and the initial delta gradient loss at the last layer. Once this is received, the forward pass and backward pass can be completed with just intermediate group boundary synchronization, which is a much smaller overhead.

Each task and device requires access to a complete copy of all filters. In order to update the filter weights during back-propagation, partial weight gradients computed by each task for each tile must be summed across all tiles to get the final weight updates. This requires the devices to communicate their entire partial weight update sets with each other or a common central device for summing at the end of the training cycle for each batch. Such weight updates are only required once at the end of each batch, and can stay local on each tile until then. For the early feature-map dominated layers, filters are relatively small and storing local copies in each device as well as communicating updates between tiles carries a small overhead in comparison to the computation and memory benefits we get from feature and gradient map partitioning.

4   Distributed Training

In the following, we describe details of our distributed tiling approach for a single layer followed by a discussion of fusing and grouping across multiple layers.

4.1   Single-Layer Tiling

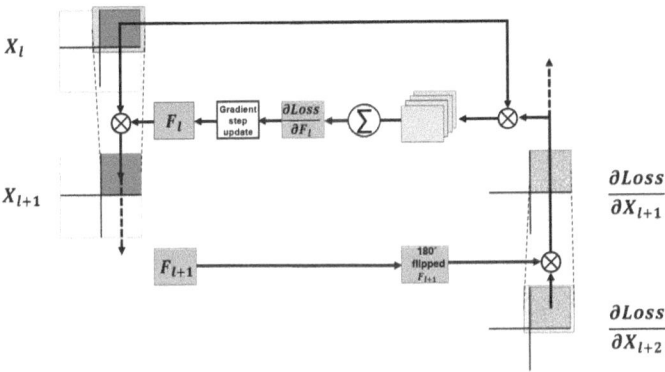

Fig. 2. Single-layer tiled forward inference and back-propagation.

Figure 2 illustrates the tiling process of a forward pass, backward pass and weight update at layer l for a 2×2 tile partition. X_l and X_{l+1} are the input and output feature maps of layer l, respectively. Assuming a tiling into an NxM grid, in the forward pass, each of the tiles in X_l with the necessary boundary data are convolved with the filter F_l to produce the NxM tiled output feature-maps X_{l+1}.

For back-propagation, we need to compute two gradients, the delta loss gradients and the weight updates. The delta loss gradients are obtained through recursive back-propagation starting with the loss gradients at the output of the last layer. To calculate the loss gradients $\frac{\partial Loss}{X_{l+1}}$, each output tile of the next layer's loss gradients, $\frac{\partial Loss}{X_{l+2}}$, together with the necessary boundary data is convolved with the 180° rotated filter to produce the corresponding tile in $\frac{\partial Loss}{X_{l+1}}$.

Finally, to compute the weight updates, the feature map tiles of X_l are first convolved with the corresponding tiles of the delta loss gradient $\frac{\partial Loss}{X_{l+1}}$ to produce NxM filter gradient sets, one for each tile. These NxM weight updates are partial sums pertaining to the region of the map the tile is associated with, and the final weight gradients $\frac{\partial Loss}{F_l}$ can simply be obtained by summing them up.

This final gradient can then be used to update F_l as illustrated in the figure. The summation requires each device to communicate their partial sums to a common device that performs the summation and transmits the updated weight gradients back to each tile. To minimize overhead, the summation can be done once for all filters in all layers at the end of the training cycle of a single batch.

4.2   Fusing and Grouping

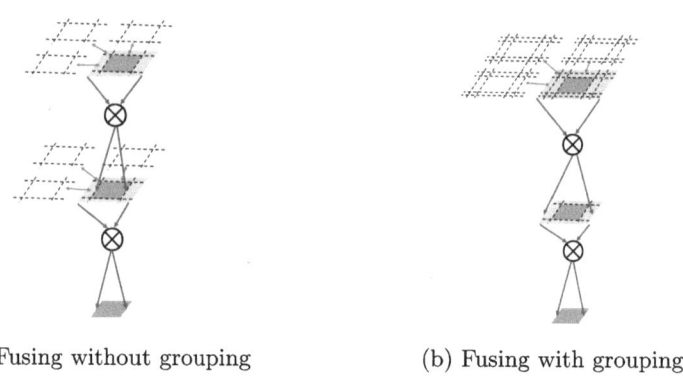

(a) Fusing without grouping   (b) Fusing with grouping

Fig. 3. Fusing and grouping illustration.

As introduced earlier, matching tile partitions in the forward and backward passes are fused across all convolutional and pooling layers in that they stay local on the same device. Figure 3 illustrates the fusing and grouping across 2 layers for a forward pass (the backward pass is symmetrical). The center region of each tile (dark green) is fused across layers, stays local on the device and is never exchanged with other devices (in both forward and backward passes). However, the devices also exchange some neighboring boundary data (light green portion) required to complete the convolutions/pooling. Figure 3(a) shows the case without grouping where boundary exchange occurs at the input to both layers thus having minimal redundant computation and storage. By contrast, Fig. 3(b) shows the case where the exchange only occurs at the input to first layer. However, in this case, the amount of shared boundary data per tile increases leading to more storage and redundant computation on each tile. In other words, grouping reduces the redundant computation and storage at the expense of additional communication and synchronization overhead, i.e. there is a trade-off between computation and communication.

Figure 4 illustrates a granular view of communication at the group boundary. Each device both transmits and receives the required boundary data to/from up to 8 neighboring tiles, where devices transmit data from the internal border of the locally computed tile while receiving boundary data external to it. These exchanges happen at the group input layers in forward and backward passes.

The double ended arrows at the feature map in device 1 indicate that similar exchanges occur with the other 7 neighboring tiles, if present. The same happens at group input delta maps and feature maps across all tiles.

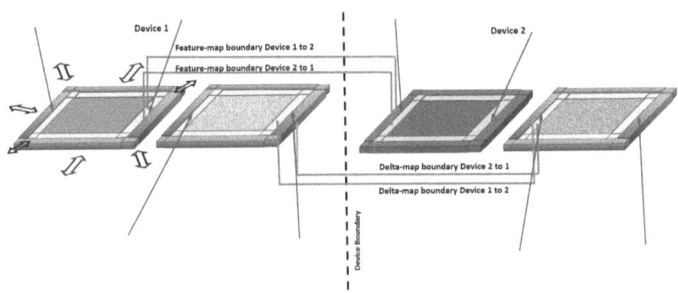

Fig. 4. Group boundary communication illustration.

The span of each tile (i, j) with boundary data at layer l can be represented by its top-left $(x1_{l,(i,j)}, y1_{l,(i,j)})$ and bottom-right $(x2_{l,(i,j)}, y2_{l,(i,j)})$ co-ordinates. Furthermore, we represent the filter/kernel size and stride at layer l as $K_l \times K_l$ and S_l, respectively. A group starting at the input to layer s and ending at the input to layer e (output of layer $e - 1$) is represented as a tuple (s, e).

Suppose we have a grid of tiles and want to create the grouping profile in the forward pass. To derive required boundary and tile data, we begin at the feature-map output of the last layer of the last group and recursively traverse backward among intermediate layers and groups. For any group, (s, e), the feature map output of the last layer of the group, e, is partitioned length and breadth wise equally among the tiles. Then, we recursively compute the dependent region in the previous layers to produce the required feature map for each tile in each intermediate layer l within the group, where $s < l \leq e$. Given the tile co-ordinates at the input to layer l (output of layer $l - 1$), the required tile region at the input to layer $l - 1$ is

$$x1_{l-1,(i,j)} = x1_{l,(i,j)} \times S_{l-1} - \lfloor \frac{K_{l-1}}{2} \rfloor \tag{1a}$$

$$y1_{l-1,(i,j)} = y1_{l,(i,j)} \times S_{l-1} - \lfloor \frac{K_{l-1}}{2} \rfloor \tag{1b}$$

$$x2_{l-1,(i,j)} = x2_{l,(i,j)} \times S_{l-1} + \lfloor \frac{K_{l-1}}{2} \rfloor + (S_{l-1} - 1) \tag{1c}$$

$$y2_{l-1,(i,j)} = y2_{l,(i,j)} \times S_{l-1} + \lfloor \frac{K_{l-1}}{2} \rfloor + (S_{l-1} - 1) \tag{1d}$$

for convolutional layer $l - 1$.

For the backward pass, computing group boundary data bounds is similar except that we go in the opposite direction, i.e. we start computing the co-ordinates from the delta gradient map output of the first layer of the network.

For any group, (s, e), given the tile co-ordinates of the delta map at intermediate layer l, where $s \leq l < e$, the tile co-ordinates of the delta map at layer $l + 1$ are

$$x1_{l+1,(i,j)} = \lceil \frac{x1_{l,(i,j)} - \lfloor \frac{K_l}{2} \rfloor}{S_l} \rceil \tag{2a}$$

$$y1_{l+1,(i,j)} = \lceil \frac{y1_{l,(i,j)} - \lfloor \frac{K_l}{2} \rfloor}{S_l} \rceil \tag{2b}$$

$$x2_{l+1,(i,j)} = \lfloor \frac{x2_{l,(i,j)} + \lfloor \frac{K_l}{2} \rfloor}{S_l} \rfloor \tag{2c}$$

$$y2_{l+1,(i,j)} = \lfloor \frac{y2_{l,(i,j)} + \lfloor \frac{K_l}{2} \rfloor}{S_l} \rfloor \tag{2d}$$

for convolutional layer l.

After completing the forward and backward passes, the partial filter gradients are computed by convolving the corresponding delta gradients with the feature-maps as described in Sect. 4.1. For this, just $\lceil \frac{K_l}{2} \rceil$ element wide boundary data would be required in the feature-map at layer l. However, this data is already gathered during the forward pass and can be re-used to avoid additional communication for this step.

5   Experiments and Results

We implemented our distributed training approach in C on top of the Darknet framework and validated our model using the first 16 layers of the Yolov2 CNN. A reference implementation is available at [20]. Our primary experimental test-bed consisted of 6 Raspberry-Pi3 devices with quad-core ARM Cortex-A53 CPUs and 1 GB of RAM each running a Linux kernel. Each tile was executed as an individual Linux process and we allocated upto 4 tiles per device to run on the 4 cores. The devices were all part of a local 100Mbps Ethernet network. For communication between processes within the same device, we used shared memory and local sockets to minimize overhead. TCP network sockets were used to communicate between processes across devices on the network. More details and results can be found in [21].

5.1   Speedup

Figure 5 shows the execution times for a single training sample (batch size of 1) across different combinations of devices and cores ranging from 1 to 6 devices, each using 1 to 4 of their cores. The number of tiles in a given device/core combination is the total number of cores across all devices. Each tile was scheduled as an independent process. Results are broken down into execution times for back-propagation and forward inference computations, communication times for filter weight updates and boundary data exchanges, and input/output communication overheads. A single device with 1 tile (1 process - single core) took around 7 min

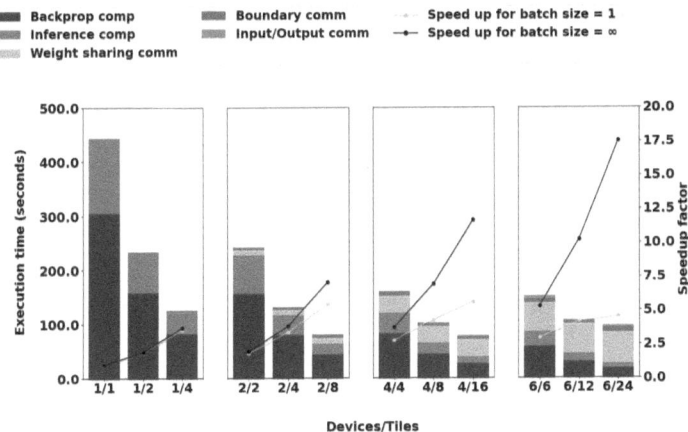

Fig. 5. Execution time split and speedup with number of tiles and devices.

to finish the training cycle (forward pass, backward pass and weight updates) on a single sample. The speedup for the different configurations are shown with respect to this baseline. Since filter weight updates are only done once per batch, we show 2 speedup factors for a baseline batch size of 1, where weight communication overhead dominates, and for infinite batch size where weight update cost is negligible compared to other components and excluded. The actual speedup should be between these 2 depending on the batch size.

We observe that computation times dominate for small number of devices and tiles, but scale down with increasing number of devices and cores (more tiles). Due to the shared memory implementation within devices, there is no overhead for communication between tiles on the same device. Consequently, the communication overhead is uniform across different numbers of cores with the same number of devices. However, boundary data and weight communication overhead increases with more devices, where overhead for weight updates dominates for a larger number of devices. This limits speedup for small batch sizes and can outweigh savings in computation times, where 6 devices perform worse than 4. At the same time, we do observe strong scaling in the speedup for large batch sizes. We will further analyze results with varying batch size later.

5.2 Memory

Figure 6 shows the peak physical memory utilization per tile measured while the training cycle of a single sample on the Raspberry-Pis was in progress. The figure also shows the split of the major memory usage components - feature maps, delta maps, filters and other implementation-related components such as a preallocated buffer for intermediate computation, communication buffers and code space. The memory consumption is ~400 MB per tile and drops to ~50 MB per tile when using 24 tiles. In general, by tiling in a finer granularity, memory

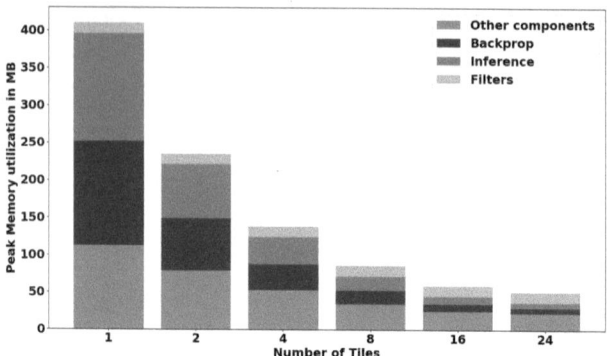

Fig. 6. Memory utilization with number of tiles.

requirements per tile and hence per device are reduced. However, while memory requirements for feature, delta maps and other buffers decreases linearly with the number of tiles, filter memory usage is constant leading to diminishing returns.

5.3   Batching and Grouping

We further conducted experiments on a batch of samples of various sizes. We also performed a comparison between grouping profiles - with and without grouping. Figure 7 shows the result of running the training cycle on a batch size of 1 to 8 samples. We conducted this experiment using all 4 cores on the 6 Rapberry Pi devices using 24 tiles. We observe that synchronizing every layer (no grouping) performs significantly better than with grouping across all batch sizes. In case of the Raspberry Pis, total execution time is dominated by computation times or weight updates, and the improvement comes from optimization of computation. Computation costs scale proportionally with the number of samples in the batch, but the filter updates are done once per batch and take roughly the same time across batch sizes. As such, the relative contribution of weight update costs decreases with larger batches. At the same time, the boundary communication and input/output communication overhead increases with larger batch size, but is negligible compared to computation cost. Overall, Raspberry-Pi devices are computation limited and hence the synchronizing at every layer to minimize redundant computation is optimal.

5.4   GPU Experiments

We also conducted experiments on a pair of Nvidia-Jetson Nano boards to illustrate the case of a communication-limited setup. Each board had a quad-core ARM Cortex-A57 CPU and a Maxwell architecture GPU with 128 CUDA cores. The 2 boards were connected using a 10Gbps Ethernet link.

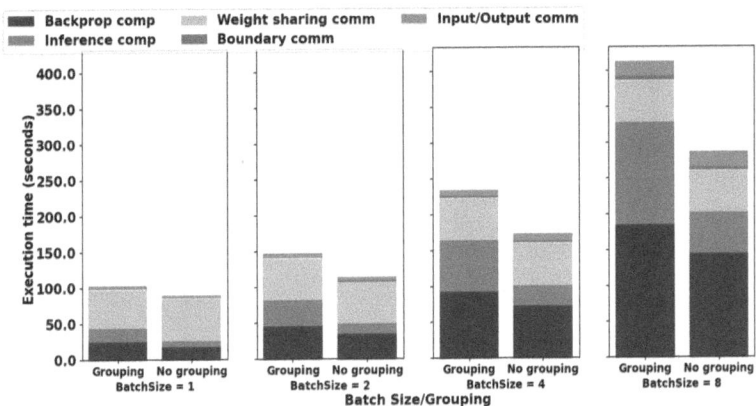

Fig. 7. Comparison with batch size and grouping.

Figure 8 illustrates the single batch training cycle time for different batch sizes for a 2-tile setup (each board training on the GPU). On the GPUs, the inference plus backprop computation is much faster than on the Pis, thus making communication and synchronization overhead the limiting factor. In this case, the difference in boundary communication overhead among different groupings though small is noticeable. The case of with grouping performs better than without grouping since it synchronizes less frequently. On the GPUs, the extra redundant computation in the grouping case has negligible effect on computation time. By contrast, the extra communication and frequent synchronization, which includes transferring data to and from the GPU incurs a relatively larger overhead. Hence, it is more optimal to synchronize less frequently, and grouping is optimal.

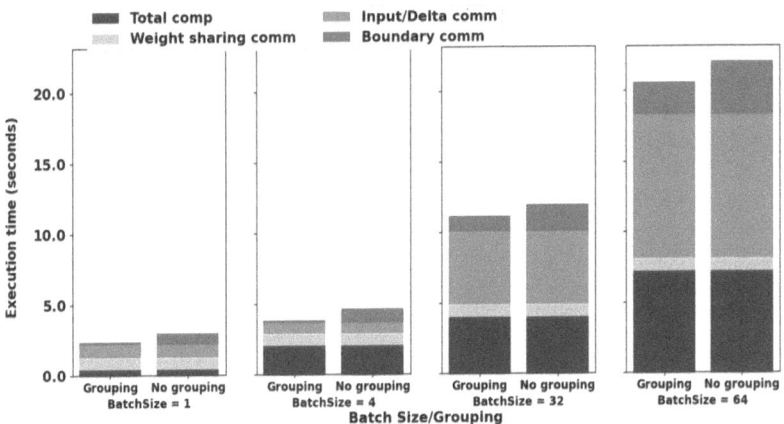

Fig. 8. 2-tile experiment with GPUs.

6   Summary and Conclusions

In this paper, we proposed a method for distributed mobile and edge training in feature-map dominated convolutional and pooling layers. Our method exploits locality in convolutional layers to partition feature maps and the delta gradients in forward and backward passes. It parallelizes training at a granular level within each sample. All intermediate layers are fused in that the core feature maps and delta maps remain local on the device with only a small overhead of shared data communication between neighboring tiles. Layers are further grouped based on a grouping profile that affects tradeoffs between computation, shared boundary communication and synchronization overhead. A grouping optimization algorithm including cost model and additional results are discussed in [21]. A reference implementation of our approach is available at [20]. Future work will explore weight partitioning techniques and how to extend our approach to other weight-dominated layers.

References

1. Ren, W., et al.: A survey on collaborative DNN inference for edge intelligence. *arXiv preprint* arXiv:2207.07812 (2022)
2. Yousefpour et al.: All one needs to know about fog computing and related edge computing paradigms: a complete survey. JSA **98**, 289–330 (2019)
3. Stahl, R., Hoffman, A., Mueller-Gritschneder, D., Gerstlauer, A., Schlichtmann, U.: DeeperThings: fully distributed CNN Inference on resource-constrained edge devices. Int. J. Parallel Prog. **49**(4), 600–624 (2021). https://doi.org/10.1007/s10766-021-00712-3
4. Zhou, L., et al.: Adaptive parallel execution of deep neural networks on heterogeneous edge devices. In: SEC (2019)
5. Du, J., et al.: A distributed in-situ CNN inference system for IoT applications. In: ICCD (2020)
6. Li, T., et al.: Federated learning: challenges, methods, and future directions. IEEE Signal Process. Mag. **37**(3), 50–60 (2020)
7. Zhao, Z., et al.: DeepThings: distributed adaptive deep learning inference on resource-constrained IoT edge clusters. IEEE TCAD **37**(11), 2348–2359 (2018)
8. Mao, J., et al.: MoDNN: local distributed mobile computing system for deep neural network. In: DATE (2017)
9. Zhang, S., et al.: DeepSlicing: collaborative and adaptive CNN inference with low latency. IEEE TPDS **32**(9), 2175–2187 (2021)
10. Alwani, M., et al.: Fused-layer CNN accelerators. In: MICRO (2016)
11. Stahl, R., et al.: Fused depthwise tiling for memory optimization in TinyML deep neural network inference. In: TinyML Research Symposium (2023)
12. Wang, Z., et al.: CoopFL: accelerating federated learning with dnn partitioning and offloading in heterogeneous edge computing. Comput. Netw. **220** (2023)
13. Sen, T., Shen, H.: Distributed training for deep learning models on an edge computing network using shielded reinforcement learning. In: ICDCS (2022)
14. Ray, P.P.: A review on TinyML: state-of-the-art and prospects. JKSUCI **34**(4), 1595–1623 (2022)

15. Grau, M.M., et al.: On-device training of machine learning models on microcontrollers with a look at federated learning. In: GoodIT (2021)
16. Lin, J., et al.: On-device training under 256KB memory. In: NeurIPS (2022)
17. Cai, H., et al.: TinyTL: reduce activations, not trainable parameters for efficient on-device learning. In: NeurIPS (2020)
18. Chiang, H.-Y., et al.: MobileTL: on-device transfer learning with inverted residual blocks. In: AAAI/IAAI/EAAI (2023)
19. Chen, Y., et al.: Exploring the use of synthetic gradients for distributed deep learning across cloud and edge resources. In: HotEdge (2019)
20. http://github.com/SLAM-Lab/Dist-CNN-Training
21. Rama, P., et al.: Distributed convolutional neural network training on resource-constrained mobile and edge clusters, UT Austin, Technical Report, UT-CERC-24-02, May 2024

Digital Twins and Smart Environments for Autonomous and Urban Systems

Autonomous Driving Pedestrian Analysis: A Digital Twin Approach Using Raspberry Pi and CARLA Simulator via MQTT

Narmada Ambigapathy$^{(\boxtimes)}$, Fatima Idrees$^{(\boxtimes)}$, Katrin Glöwing$^{(\boxtimes)}$,
Charles Steinmetz$^{(\boxtimes)}$, and Achim Rettberg$^{(\boxtimes)}$

Hamm-Lippstadt University of Applied Sciences, Lippstadt, Germany
{`narmada.ambigapathy,fatima.idrees,katrin.gloewing,charles.steinmetz,`
`achim.rettberg`}`@hshl.de`

Abstract. In this paper, we present a novel digital twin framework for pedestrian analysis in autonomous driving. The digital twin replicates real-world systems, enabling the monitoring, simulation, and analysis of pedestrian detection algorithms in a controlled environment. Our framework integrates the YOLOv9 model on a Raspberry Pi, enhanced by a Movidius Neural Compute Stick, to detect pedestrians and transmit data via MQTT to the CARLA Simulator. Additionally, we have integrated MediaPipe with YOLOv9 to detect pedestrian poses, such as walking, standing, or unknown, and mirrored these behaviors in CARLA. If discrepancies are detected, feedback is sent to the Raspberry Pi to enable potential corrections. This setup allows extensive testing across diverse scenarios, improving the safety and reliability of autonomous vehicles. To validate the proposed approach, we developed a use case and compared execution times for the detection algorithm on Raspberry Pi 5, with and without the Movidius Neural Compute Stick. Our study details the system architecture and implementation, highlighting significant advancements in pedestrian analysis for autonomous driving technologies.

Keywords: Digital Twin · Autonomous Driving · Object Detection · YOLO · MQTT · CARLA Simulator · Embedded Systems

1 Introduction

The concept of digital twins, virtual models of physical systems enabling online monitoring, simulation, and analysis, has significantly advanced autonomous driving technologies [1]. Digital twins facilitate detailed testing and validation of vehicle systems, particularly in complex urban environments where unpredictable pedestrian behavior poses challenges [2]. Current pedestrian detection solutions often lack dynamic feedback systems for continuous testing and online analysis. This research addresses that gap by introducing a framework for continuous monitoring and validation of pedestrian behavior. Our framework allows autonomous driving systems to test a variety of scenarios before being deployed in real-world environments.

© IFIP International Federation for Information Processing 2026
Published by Springer Nature Switzerland AG 2026
M. A. Wehrmeister et al. (Eds.): IESS 2024, IFIP AICT 760, pp. 77–88, 2026.
https://doi.org/10.1007/978-3-032-07102-6_7

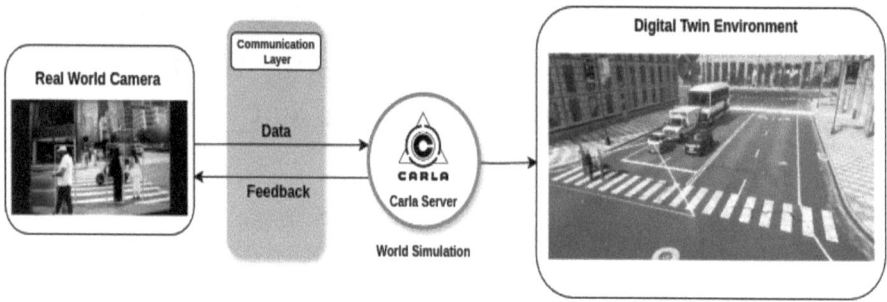

Fig. 1. Overview of Digital Twin approach

The proposed digital twin framework integrates real-world pedestrian detection with simulated feedback, improving vehicle safety and reliability. The framework integrates three key technologies: the YOLO (You Only Look Once) [3] model, MQTT (Message Queuing Telemetry Transport)[1], and the CARLA Simulator[2] as illustrated in Fig. 1. YOLO runs on a Raspberry Pi to detect pedestrians, while MQTT facilitates data exchange between the physical system and the CARLA-based digital twin to test in a simulated urban environment. MediaPipe is integrated with YOLOv9 to analyze pedestrian poses, with feedback sent to the Raspberry Pi if deviations occur.

The paper reviews related work in Sect. 2. Section 3 details the system architecture and the implementation details, including the integration of YOLOv9, MQTT, and CARLA. Section 4 presents the evaluation results. The Sect. 5 explores potential applications, and the paper concludes in Sect. 6 with findings and suggestions for future research.

2   Related Work

Pedestrian detection and analysis in autonomous driving play a critical role in ensuring both the safety and development of such systems. This section reviews recent developments and methodologies in this area, focusing on convolutional neural networks (CNNs) [4], object detection models based on YOLO [5], and the concept of digital twins, particularly in the domain of autonomous driving using CARLA [6] as a simulator. The literature on pedestrian detection in autonomous driving has evolved significantly with the use of CNNs, notably YOLO models. CNNs have consistently outperformed traditional methods for image recognition, particularly in autonomous driving. Agnihotri et al. (2019) [7] demonstrated the feasibility of using a Raspberry Pi for low-cost autonomous systems, showing how CNNs could map camera inputs to steering commands. This system highlighted the viability of using cost-effective hardware like the Raspberry Pi for complex tasks such as image processing and motor control in autonomous vehicles.

---

[1] https://mqtt.org.
[2] https://carla.org.

The YOLO family of algorithms is renowned for its object detection capabilities due to its speed and accuracy. Wu et al. (2021) [8] introduced YOLO v5-Ghost, which reduced computational complexity while maintaining high detection accuracy. This innovation employed Ghost modules to replace standard convolutions, making it suitable for embedded systems like the Raspberry Pi. Further advancements in YOLO were made by Wang et al. (2024) [9], with YOLOv9 introducing Programmable Gradient Information (PGI) and the Generalized Efficient Layer Aggregation Network (GELAN). These developments addressed key issues such as information bottlenecks and provided superior performance on the MS COCO dataset.

However, despite these advancements, existing approaches often lack dynamic, online feedback mechanisms between physical and digital systems. Niranjan et al. (2021) [10] leveraged CARLA to develop and test object detection models, emphasizing the importance of simulation in generating and labeling large datasets for training autonomous driving models. Digital twins (DT) have emerged as a key concept in autonomous driving, offering opportunities for testing and validation in simulated environments. Steinmetz et al. (2022) [11] used Node-RED and CARLA simulators to model and simulate DT-based systems, providing a platform for continuously updating digital twin models with real-world data, thus bridging the gap between simulation and real-world.

Our work differentiates itself by integrating MediaPipe with YOLOv9 for not only pedestrian detection but also pose analysis (walking, standing, or unknown). Furthermore, this study incorporates online feedback from the CARLA digital twin, providing a stable system for urban driving scenarios where unpredictable pedestrian behavior can pose significant challenges. By addressing the gap of feedback-driven systems, our framework enhances the safety and reliability of autonomous driving systems by dynamically correcting pedestrian behavior.

3 System Architecture and Implementation

This section outlines the integrated framework of the proposed digital twin system for pedestrian detection and behavior analysis in autonomous driving. It combines the physical and digital components and includes a feedback system that enhances reliable communication and adaptability.

3.1 Overview of System Architecture

The proposed framework consists of a physical system, a communication layer, and a digital twin environment, each playing a crucial role in pedestrian detection and behavior analysis. The architecture is designed to ensure object detection using the YOLOv9 model running on a Raspberry Pi, with MediaPipe for analyzing pedestrian poses. An MQTT broker facilitates data communication between the physical system and the CARLA Simulator, which is used to replicate real-world scenarios and validate system performance that as depicted in Fig. 2.

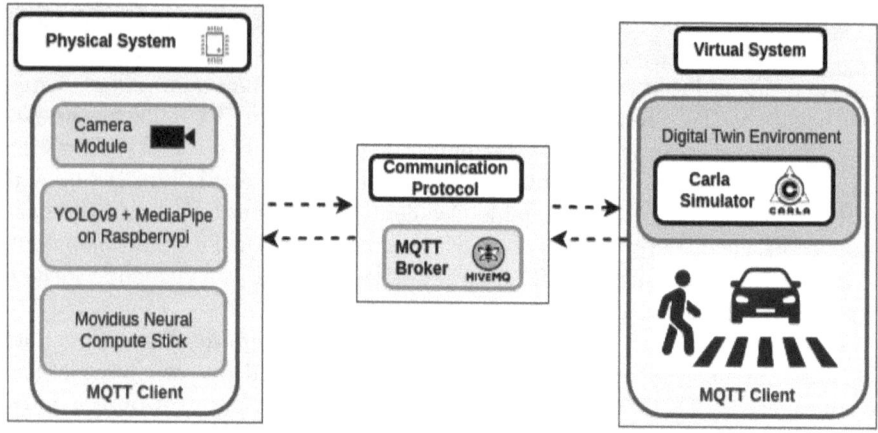

Fig. 2. Overview of System architecture.

3.2 System Design and Tooling

The system integrates both hardware and software components to ensure the pedestrian detection, behavior analysis, and simulation for the framework, as shown in the UML activity diagram in Fig. 3.

The core hardware includes a **Raspberry Pi 5** with a **Movidius Neural Compute Stick** (NCS) for accelerating inference and a camera module for capturing online video feeds. The Raspberry Pi runs the YOLOv9 model for object detection and MediaPipe for pedestrian pose analysis.

On the software side, the **Raspberry Pi OS** provides the development environment, with **OpenCV** handling image processing. Data from the physical system (pedestrian count and behavior) is transmitted via the **Mosquitto MQTT broker** to the **CARLA Simulator**, which simulates real-world scenarios. The CARLA Python API is used for controlling the simulation and mirroring pedestrian actions in the digital twin environment. Libraries such as paho-mqtt facilitate MQTT communication between the Raspberry Pi and the CARLA system. The workflow is streamlined as follows:

- **Pedestrian Detection & Analysis:** The camera captures video, processed by YOLOv9 and MediaPipe, which outputs pedestrian count and behavior.
- **Data Transmission:** Detected data is sent to the MQTT broker, where it is published to CARLA for online simulation.
- **Digital Twin Simulation:** CARLA replicates the physical system by spawning virtual pedestrians based on the transmitted data. If abnormal behaviors are detected (e.g., unexpected stops), feedback is sent from CARLA to the Raspberry Pi via MQTT, enabling online adaptations.

This integrated design ensures efficient framework for communication, behavior analysis, and online feedback, providing a stable environment for testing and validating pedestrian detection systems for addressing potential risks in autonomous driving systems dynamically.

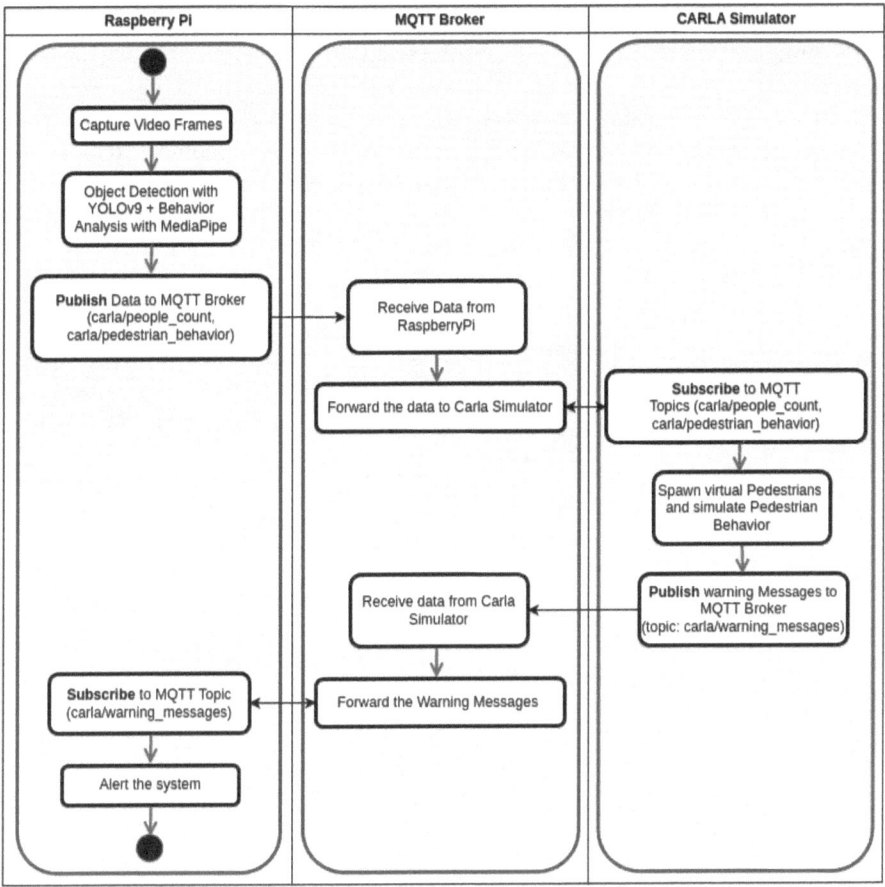

Fig. 3. UML Activity Diagram for Proposed Digital Twin Framework.

3.3   Physical System: Raspberry Pi with YOLO Object Detection

The physical system is centered around a Raspberry Pi 5, augmented with a Movidius Neural Compute Stick (NCS) [12], which provides a hardware system to execute the YOLOv9 object detection algorithm. The NCS connects to the host machine over a USB 2.0 High Speed interface and can be plugged directly into a USB port on the host machine or into a USB hub connected to the host machine. The setup is aimed at online video frame capturing and processing. The camera module connected to the Raspberry Pi captures video frames, which are then fed into the YOLOv9 model pre-trained on the COCO dataset.

MediaPipe is integrated to detect the pose of pedestrians and output their behavior (walking/ standing/ unknown) along with the counts. The Movidius Neural Compute Stick provides an additional computational boost, enhancing the inference speed and performance of the YOLOv9 model. The Raspberry Pi, running on the Raspbian OS, utilizes the Neural Compute SDK (NCSDK) to seamlessly integrate and accelerate deep learning processes. This reliable hardware configuration ensures optimized processing of video frames, allowing accurate detection, pose estimation, behavior analysis, and counting of detected pedestrians. The workflow involves capturing video frames, processing them through the YOLOv9 and MediaPipe models to detect people, extract their pose and behavior. This outputs the count and behavior as integer and string values, which are logged and passed for transmission via the communication layer respectively. Figure 4 depicts the flow of this physical system.

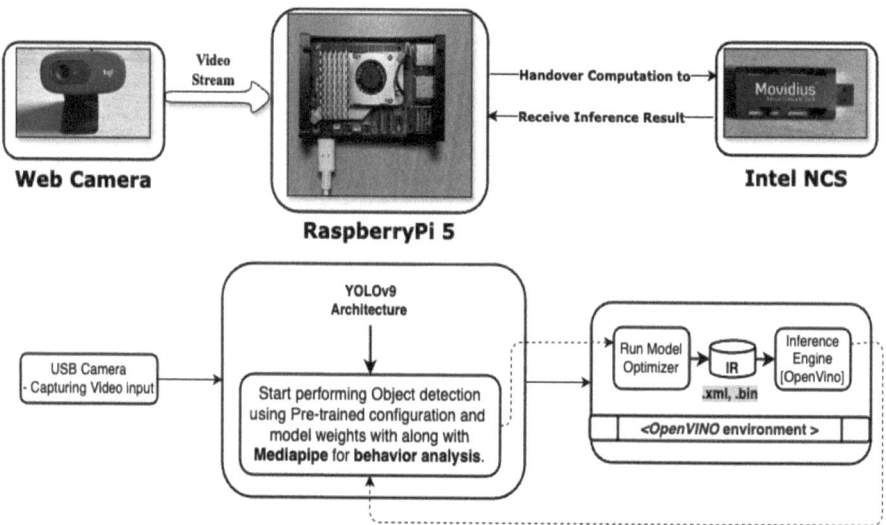

Fig. 4. Hardware setup and workflow for the physical system.

3.4   Communication Layer: MQTT Broker Setup

The communication layer is an integral component for facilitating the interaction between the Raspberry Pi and the CARLA Simulator as shown in the Fig. 5. An MQTT broker, such as Mosquitto, is configured on a server accessible to both the Raspberry Pi and the CARLA Simulator. The system utilizes several specific MQTT topics to streamline data transmission. For example, the topic_1 is used for sending the detected people count from the Raspberry Pi to the MQTT broker. The topic_2 is employed to convey the behavior of pedestrians to the CARLA Simulator. In response, the CARLA Simulator can send messages back to the real-world camera using the topic_3, alerting the autonomous system if a pedestrian is not acting appropriately. This setup establishes a stable data transmission path, ensuring seamless communication of object detection results and behavioral information from the physical system to the digital twin, and vice versa.

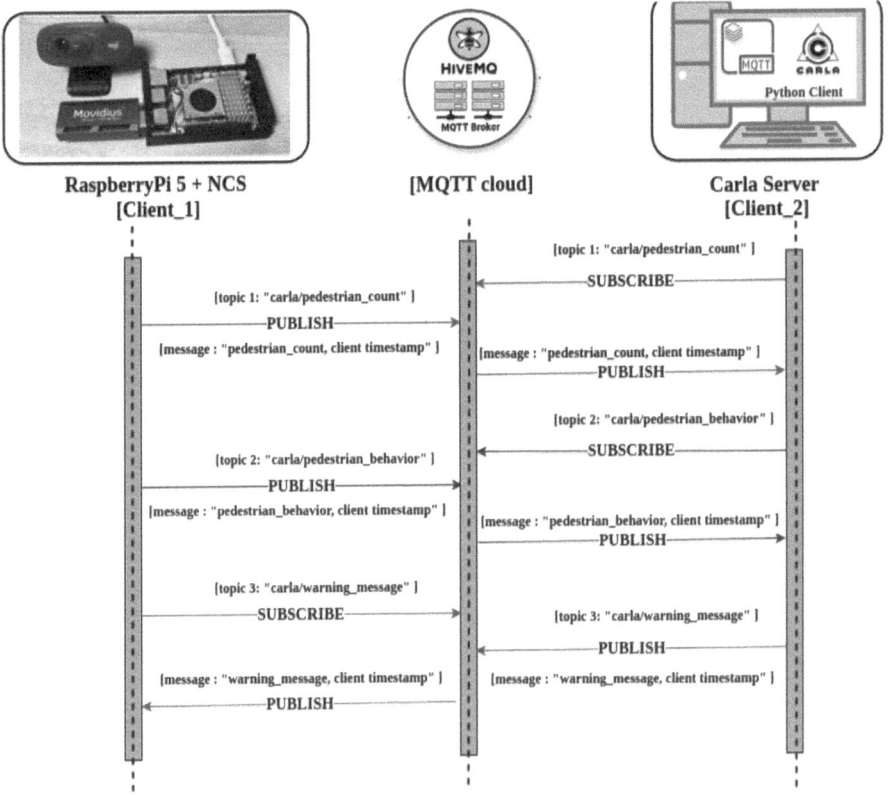

Fig. 5. Communication layer setup.

3.5 Digital Twin and Feedback System: Integration with CARLA Simulator

The digital twin of the physical system is created through the integration of the CARLA Simulator. The CARLA Simulator subscribes to the MQTT topics defined in the communication layer. Upon receiving the people count from the Raspberry Pi, a corresponding number of virtual people is spawned in the CARLA Simulator. This integration effectively mirrors the physical detection scenario in a simulated setting, allowing for extensive testing and validation under controlled conditions. The CARLA client communicates with the CARLA server via an API [13], utilizing functions such as GetMap, GetBlueprintLibrary, TrySpawnActor, and SpawnActor to accurately reflect real-world detections within the simulation, as depicted in Fig. 6. To ensure the virtual pedestrians behave realistically, WalkerControl is used to simulate pedestrian actions, mirroring the behaviors observed by the physical system. By combining the YOLOv9 object detection model and MediaPipe pose estimation with efficient communication via MQTT, the system achieves a comprehensive and adaptive digital twin that accurately responds to real-world conditions.

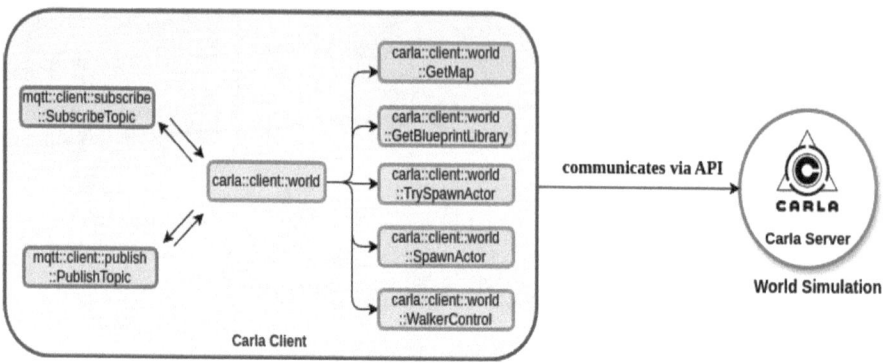

Fig. 6. Digital twin integration.

A critical component of this framework is the **feedback system**, which facilitates online communication between the CARLA simulator and the physical system. By continuously monitoring pedestrian behavior, the CARLA simulator sends alerts to the Raspberry Pi via the MQTT broker if abnormal actions, such as abrupt stops or erratic movements, are detected. This feedback enables the physical system to adjust its decision-making process in online, ensuring enhanced vehicle responsiveness and safety. The feedback mechanism is particularly valuable in handling dynamic pedestrian interactions, addressing a significant challenge faced by many existing autonomous driving systems.

4   Evaluation

The evaluation of the proposed system focuses on assessing the performance, accuracy, and practical applicability of the digital twin framework for pedestrian detection and behavior analysis. The key metrics and findings from the evaluation are summarized below:

4.1   Performance Metrics

Model Performance on Raspberry Pi 5:

- **Without Movidius:** The YOLOv9 model achieved a frame rate of 0.28 FPS, demonstrating its capability to process video frames sufficiently capable on the Raspberry Pi 5 alone for 608 × 608 resolution .
- **With Movidius Neural Compute Stick:** The addition of the Movidius Neural Compute Stick significantly enhanced processing capabilities, increasing the FPS to 0.15 and improving overall inference speed and performance.
- **With MediaPipe Integration:** When integrating MediaPipe for behavior analysis with YOLOv9, the combined system achieved 0.17 FPS. This configuration provides not only pedestrian detection but also behavior analysis, balancing speed and accuracy effectively (Table 1).

Table 1. Performance comparison of YOLOv9 with and without MediaPipe on Raspberry Pi 5, with and without Movidius Neural Compute Stick.

Configuration	FPS (YOLOv9 Only)	FPS (YOLOv9 + MediaPipe)
Raspberry Pi 5 (No Movidius)	0.28	0.31
Raspberry Pi 5 + Movidius	0.15	0.17

4.2   Accuracy of Pedestrian Detection

- **Detection Accuracy:** The YOLOv9 model demonstrated good accuracy in detecting pedestrians, with effective counting and behavior classification (walking, standing, or unknown) when combined with MediaPipe. The system was able to accurately reflect real-world pedestrian scenarios within the CARLA Simulator.
- **Simulation Fidelity:** The CARLA Simulator accurately mirrored real-world scenarios by spawning virtual pedestrians based on detected counts and behaviors. This online updating capability is crucial for testing and validation within simulated environments.

4.3   Real-World Testing

Detection and Behavior Analysis Instances

To demonstrate the effectiveness of the proposed framework, various instances were analyzed from a continuous video feed. Two distinct test instances will be highlighted as an example in the section.

Test Instance 1. As illustrated in Fig. 7, the YOLOv9 model successfully detected multiple pedestrians crossing the street. This data, including pedestrian count and behavior, was transmitted to the CARLA Simulator via MQTT. The CARLA Simulator then spawned virtual pedestrians to replicate the real-world scenario accurately.

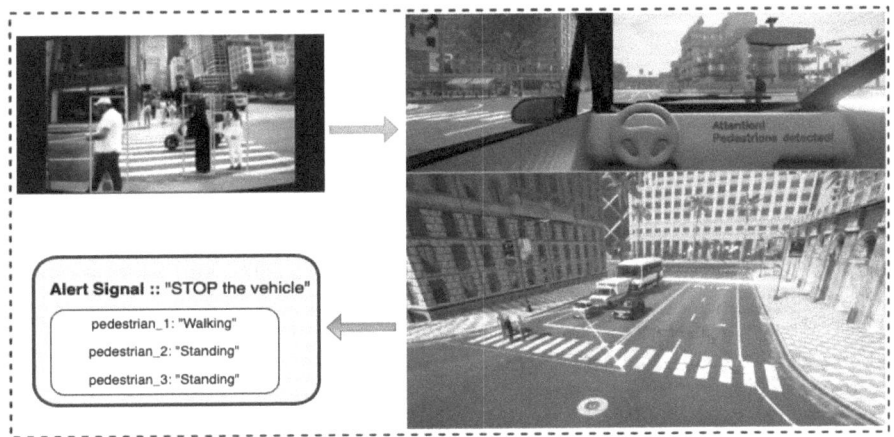

Fig. 7. Test Instance 1: No Warning signal passed.

During this instance, all pedestrians were in "walker" mode within CARLA, and no warning messages were triggered. The vehicle actor in the CARLA maintained its current state, with no changes, until a signal or state change occurred. This test case demonstrated the system's ability to perform accurate online detection and simulation, reflecting real-world pedestrian behavior effectively.

Test Instance 2. In the second test case, shown in Fig. 8, the YOLOv9 model identified two pedestrians standing still in the street. This detection data, including the pedestrians' status, is transmitted to the CARLA Simulator via MQTT. In response, the simulator displayed the two virtual pedestrians in a standing pose. Upon receiving this information, the system triggered a warning message indicating that the vehicle actor in the CARLA simulation should stop. Consequently, the simulated vehicle halted its movement until a signal or state change was detected, demonstrating the system's capability to react to specific pedestrian behaviors and adapt its actions accordingly.

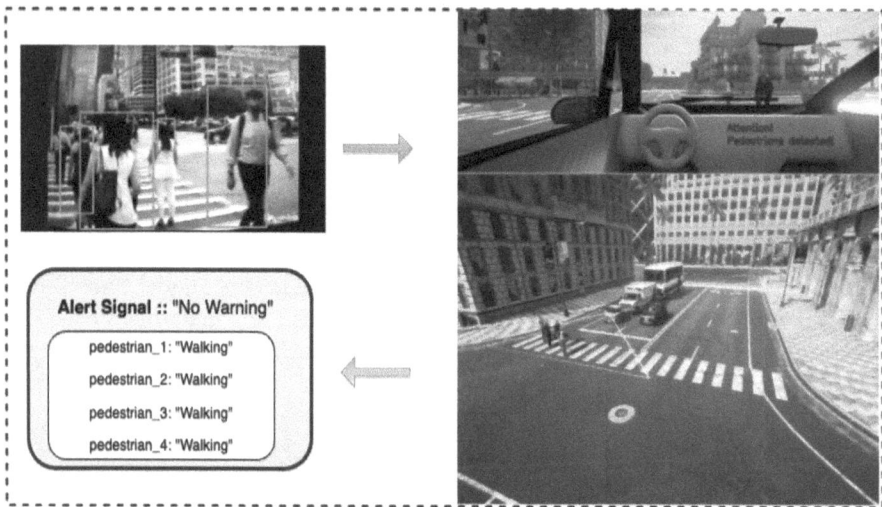

Fig. 8. Test Instance 2: Warning signal passed.

5　Applications and Use Cases

The proposed digital twin framework for pedestrian detection in autonomous driving offers several key applications and use cases:

- **Simulation and Testing Environment**: Integration with the CARLA Simulator enables extensive testing of the pedestrian detection system under diverse scenarios, such as varying weather and lighting conditions. This helps identify weaknesses and improve the stability of detection algorithms before real-world deployment.

- **Online Monitoring and Analytics**: The MQTT communication protocol allows for online monitoring and analysis of pedestrian detection data. This aids fleet management and urban planning by identifying potential risk areas and improving safety measures.
- **Smart City Integration**: The system can be integrated with other smart city infrastructure to enhance urban mobility. By sharing pedestrian detection data with traffic management systems and smart traffic lights, the framework can improve traffic flow and reduce congestion.
- **Synthetic Dataset Collection**: The digital twin framework facilitates the creation of synthetic datasets by simulating various pedestrian scenarios within the CARLA Simulator. These datasets can be used to train and validate pedestrian detection models, improving their accuracy and robustness without the need for extensive real-world data collection.

By addressing these applications and use cases, the proposed system contributes to broader goals of improving urban mobility and safety through innovative technological solutions.

6   Conclusion

This paper presents a comprehensive digital twin framework for pedestrian detection and behavior analysis, integrating YOLOv9 with MediaPipe and leveraging the CARLA Simulator for realistic virtual replication. The framework effectively combines reliable object detection with online behavior analysis, providing valuable insights for autonomous driving systems. The evaluation demonstrates that the framework performs effectively, with improved processing speed and detection accuracy. The integration of MediaPipe with YOLOv9 enhances the system's capabilities, balancing speed and detailed analysis. The practical applications of the system span simulation and testing, online monitoring, and smart city integration, contributing to advancements in autonomous driving technology and urban mobility. Currently, the framework uses password-protected client IDs and TLS/SSL encryption to secure MQTT communication between the Raspberry Pi and the CARLA simulator. To further improve security, future versions will include additional safety protocols like client authentication with certificates and better access control. These measures will enhance the integrity and confidentiality of the communication infrastructure, making autonomous driving technologies more reliable and safe.

Future work will focus on optimizing the system for different hardware configurations, expanding sensor integration, and refining simulation environments to further enhance robustness and real-world applicability. The study underscores the importance of digital twin approaches in developing safer and more reliable autonomous driving systems, offering a significant contribution to the field.

References

1. Rosen, R., von Wichert, G., Lo, G., Bettenhausen, K.D.: About the importance of autonomy and digital twins for the future of manufacturing. In: IFAC-PapersOnLine, vol. 48, no. 3, pp. 567-572. 15th IFAC Symposium on Information Control Problems in Manufacturing 2015. https://doi.org/10.1016/j.ifacol.2015.06.141, https://www.sciencedirect.com/science/article/pii/S2405896315003808
2. Shoukat, M. U., Yan, L., Zou, B., Zhang, J., Niaz, A., Raza, M.U.: Application of digital twin technology in the field of autonomous driving test. In: 2022 Third International Conference on Latest Trends in Electrical Engineering and Computing Technologies (INTELLECT), pp. 1–6, Karachi, Pakistan (2022). https://doi.org/10.1109/INTELLECT55495.2022.9969184
3. Redmon, J., Divvala, S., Girshick, R., Farhadi, A.: you only look once: unified, online object detection. In: Proceedings of the IEEE Conference on Computer Vision and Pattern Recognition (CVPR), June 2016
4. O'Shea, K., Nash, R.: An introduction to convolutional neural networks. CoRR, abs/1511.08458, http://arxiv.org/abs/1511.08458 (2015)
5. Liu, C., Tao, Y., Liang, J., Li, K., Chen, Y.: Object detection based on YOLO network. In: 2018 IEEE 4th Information Technology and Mechatronics Engineering Conference (ITOEC), pp. 799–803 (2018). https://doi.org/10.1109/ITOEC.2018.8740604
6. Dosovitskiy, A., Ros, G., Codevilla, F., Lopez, A., Koltun, V.: CARLA: an open urban driving simulator. In: Levine, S., Vanhoucke, V., Goldberg, K. (eds.), Proceedings of the 1st Annual Conference on Robot Learning, pp. 1–16. Proceedings of Machine Learning Research, vol. 78. PMLR (2017)
7. Agnihotri, A., Saraf, P., Bapnad, K.R.: A convolutional neural network approach towards self-driving cars. In: 2019 IEEE 16th India Council International Conference (INDICON), pp. 1–4 (2019). https://doi.org/10.1109/INDICON47234.2019.9030307
8. Wu, T.-H., Wang, T.-W., Liu, Y.-Q.: Online vehicle and distance detection based on improved yolo v5 network. In: 2021 3rd World Symposium on Artificial Intelligence (WSAI), pp. 24–28 (2021). https://doi.org/10.1109/WSAI51899.2021.9486316
9. Wang, C.-Y., Yeh, I.-H., Liao, H.-Y.M.: YOLOv9: learning what you want to learn using programmable gradient information. arXiv preprint arXiv:2402.13616, https://arxiv.org/abs/2402.13616 (2024)
10. Niranjan, D.R. and VinayKarthik, B.C.: Deep learning based object detection model for autonomous driving research using CARLA simulator. In: 2021 2nd International Conference on Smart Electronics and Communication (ICOSEC), pp. 1251–1258 (2021). https://doi.org/10.1109/ICOSEC51865.2021.9591747
11. Steinmetz, C., et al.: Digital twins modeling and simulation with node-RED and Carla. IFAC-PapersOnLine, vol. 55, no. 19, pp. 97–102. 5th IFAC Workshop on Advanced Maintenance Engineering, Services and Technologies AMEST 2022 (2022). https://doi.org/10.1016/j.ifacol.2022.09.190, https://www.sciencedirect.com/science/article/pii/S2405896322014057
12. Movidius, Neural Compute Stick (NCS) (2017). https://movidius.github.io/ncsdk/ncs.html
13. CARLA simulator python API documentation (2024). https://carla.readthedocs.io/en/latest/python_api

A Digital Twin-Based Approach for Collaborative Physical Internet in Smart Cities Using CARLA and Gaia-X

Katrin Glöwing[1]([✉]), Narmada Ambigapathy[1], Mehdi Azarafza[1],
Charles Steinmetz[1], Achim Rettberg[1], and Jonah Windolph[2]

[1] Hamm-Lippstadt University of Applied Sciences, Lippstadt, Germany
{katrin.gloewing,narmada.ambigapathy,mehdi.azarafza,
charles.steinmetz,achim.rettberg}@hshl.de
[2] Institute for Applied Informatics (InfAI), Leipzig, Germany
windolph@infai.org

Abstract. The expansion of logistics networks, driven by evolving business models, enables convenient online shopping but also poses environmental and public health challenges in urban areas. To address these issues, this paper presents an approach that integrates the Physical Internet(PI) within a Digital Twin (DT) environment. The PI is a logistics system that moves goods efficiently through standardized containers and networks. Utilizing the CARLA simulator, a prototype is developed that incorporates Gaia-X security components and a Multi-Agent System (MAS) to ensure secure and efficient freight transport. A key contribution of this work is the introduction of a new standard agent equipped with Gaia-X components, capable of representing both vehicles and parcels within the PI framework. This agent facilitates dynamic adaptation and secure exchanges at transport nodes. The extensibility of this framework allows for the inclusion of various entities, enabling real-time route optimization and enhancing overall system security. This paper showcases the current implementation and progress of this concept, providing a foundation for further testing and development in smart city logistics.

Keywords: Digital Twin (DT) · Physical Internet (PI) · Gaia-X · Smart Cities · Multi-Agent System (MAS)

1 Introduction

Advancements in logistics have enabled new business models, allowing customers to order products from home, but the expansion of transport networks can also lead to environmental and public health issues in urban areas [1]. These challenges can be mitigated through effective monitoring and connecting of transport nodes, utilizing the Physical Internet (PI) [2]. The PI's interoperable capabilities allow seamless integration across all levels of the logistics chain, from node to node [2].

A critical component of the PI is ensuring security, as parcels are exchanged between various entities that must be trusted by all involved parties [3]. To help

© IFIP International Federation for Information Processing 2026
Published by Springer Nature Switzerland AG 2026
M. A. Wehrmeister et al. (Eds.): IESS 2024, IFIP AICT 760, pp. 89–98, 2026.
https://doi.org/10.1007/978-3-032-07102-6_8

address this need, the Gaia-X framework, which provides a secure, federated data infrastructure across various sectors in Europe, promotes the use of verifiable credentials to establish trust and ensure participant identification [4].

Implementing complex PI scenarios with physical components, such as vehicles and users, is resource-intensive. This is where the concept of Digital Twin(DT) becomes essential, as it allows the simulation of various scenarios, helping to identify potential issues and develop optimal solutions before real-world deployment [5]. Furthermore, integrating a Multi-Agent System (MAS) within the PI allows autonomous agents to make local decisions, enabling dynamic route planning and optimizing the supply chain [6,7].

This paper presents a use case focused on ensuring freight transport security within the PI, leveraging Gaia-X components and MAS, and simulating the concept in the CARLA environment. The next sections provide an analysis of related work and background to establish the relevance of this approach. Following that, the paper presents the integration concept, structured around the V-model, which serves as a guide for the development process. A practical demonstration in CARLA showcases the integration of DTs and Gaia-X security components, supported by a Cloud Parcel Service that facilitates parcel delivery communication. The Vehicle Parcel Service, operating within the vehicle, serves as the interface to the broader system. The paper concludes with a summary of the results and outlines directions for future research.

2   Related Work and Background

The paradigm shift introduced by the **PI** aims to revolutionize logistics by mirroring the open and interconnected structure of digital networks. Symbolically, the PI resembles the digital Internet, comprising a vast network of interconnected physical and logical elements, hence the term "Physical Internet" [8]. The PI operates through the integration of standardized nodes, containers, movers, and protocols to manage, transport, and store parcels efficiently [2]. Specifically, the Road-Based PI (RBPI) seeks to reduce road freight traffic while maintaining equivalent transport volumes with fewer, more efficient vehicles by dynamically adjusting parcel routes [3,9]. Although promising, this innovative concept is still in its early stages, requiring further development and testing [9]. Given the complexity of the system—due to the numerous units involved, the distances covered, and the time required—simulation plays a critical role in identifying potential improvements.

In this context, **DTs** have proven instrumental in enhancing urban traffic management by providing digital representations of physical and non-physical systems [10]. DTs enable the simulation of existing or planned systems, allowing for comprehensive testing of various scenarios [5,10]. Originally presented by Michael Grieves in 2003 and published in 2014 [11], the DT concept has evolved to include multiple components—such as visualization, logic, and data processing algorithms—that together simulate both the physical and operational aspects of real-world systems [12]. Given the intricate nature of logistics networks, the ability to visualize and simulate complex scenarios using DTs becomes crucial for understanding and optimizing these systems. DTs have been applied in various contexts, such as the intelligent traffic management system in Hamburg, which integrates real-time sensor data (IoT) using the MARS multi-agent framework [13].

To further enhance decision-making within such complex systems, **MAS** are increasingly employed alongside DTs [14,15]. Mariani et al. [14,15] explore potential collaborations between agents and DT,, demonstrating how MAS can support complex simulations and decision-making processes. MAS consists of multiple autonomous agents that collaborate to solve problems more efficiently than a single agent could [16]. These systems facilitate dynamic information sharing, negotiation, and coordination among agents, allowing them to adapt in real-time to changing environments [17]. The visualization and testing of these complex, multi-agent interactions can be significantly improved through simulation platforms.

One such platform is the **CARLA Simulator**, an open-source tool widely used for assessing and training autonomous driving algorithms. CARLA offers a realistic virtual environment, making it ideal for visualizing and simulating urban logistics networks and optimizing operations [18]. Studies have utilized CARLA for various simulations, including DTs and autonomous systems [19–21]. Additionally, frameworks like MATS-Gym introduce multi-agent training environments within CARLA, generating diverse scenarios to train autonomous driving agents [22]. Therefore, CARLA not only supports the visualization of complex logistics scenarios but also facilitates the integration of MAS, enhancing the understanding and optimization of these systems.

Despite these advancements, the existing work does not consider the essential security aspects for supply chains. The integration of Gaia-X concepts for secure logistics within a PI framework remains unexplored.

Gaia-X, initiated by Germany and France, aims to establish a secure and sovereign data infrastructure for Europe. The project emphasizes secure and trustworthy data exchanges within a decentralized ecosystem, allowing participants to retain control over their data while benefiting from shared standardized infrastructure [4,23,24]. Gaia-X's principles of openness, transparency, and interoperability [4] align with the needs of modern logistics networks, but their application within the PI and DT framework has not been extensively researched. Incorporating Gaia-X principles within a Digital Twin simulation platform like CARLA could serve as a prototype for enhancing data security and trust in logistics operations.

Recent studies have begun to explore the integration of DTs and MAS within the PI context, highlighting both the benefits and challenges of such an approach [25]. However, these studies have not addressed the integration of Gaia-X concepts to enhance the security and efficiency of logistics in smart cities. This paper proposes a novel approach that combines MAS, PI, Gaia-X, and the CARLA simulator to create a DT-based transport network for urban logistics. By incorporating Gaia-X principles, this approach aims to ensure a trustworthy supply chain, addressing previously overlooked aspects in similar DT and MAS visualizations within CARLA.

3 Concept of Integration of Digital Twins and Gaia-X in Physical Internet

Research indicates a need for a deeper exploration of supply chain security within the PI framework. Given the complexity of logistics networks and dynamic supply chains involving multiple actors, Gaia-X was selected as the security framework. To address freight transport and the integration of a security concept within a DT, a simulation will be developed to model parcel deliveries and ensure security using Gaia-X components.

3.1 Method

The software development follows the V-model [26], a standard approach for both software and embedded systems development. This model progresses through increasingly detailed stages: starting with requirements analysis, then moving to system analysis and architecture, design, and finally implementation. Each stage undergoes validation or verification, with these tests represented on the right side of the V-model [26].

3.2 Requirements

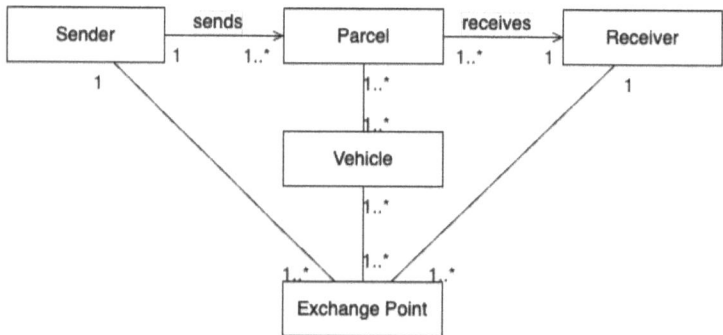

Fig. 1. Illustration of the components with notations.

This section outlines the vision and key software requirements. Figure 1 illustrates a model depicting actors, parcels, and nodes, showing scenarios where a sender may dispatch multiple parcels, a receiver may accept several at once, and vehicles may transport and forward various parcels through multiple vehicles. Exchange points for loading, reloading, and unloading parcels are included, with

Table 1. Requirements of the DT.

R1	The system shall allow a sender to send several parcels at the same time.
R2	The system shall allow a recipient to receive several parcels at the same time.
R3	The system shall enable a vehicle to transport several parcels at the same time.
R4	The system shall allow a parcel to be delivered to the recipient via several vehicles, according to the appropriate route.
R5	The system shall support the use of exchange points for loading, reloading, and unloading parcels.
R6	The system shall ensure a secure supply chain with trustworthy actors to hand over the parcels.

one being selected as needed. The following requirements for the DT concept, shown in Table 1, are derived from this vision.

The goal is to demonstrate the feasibility of simulating the PI as a DT within the CARLA environment, ensuring a trustworthy supply chain.

3.3 Analysis and Architecture

The proposed concept addresses a scenario where Person A (the sender) needs to send a parcel to Person B (the receiver) over a significant distance, requiring substantial resources. Person A registers the parcel, and the system uses logic to identify a suitable vehicle that is already planning a partially similar route. This vehicle, equipped with Gaia-X services, is selected for reliable delivery and is

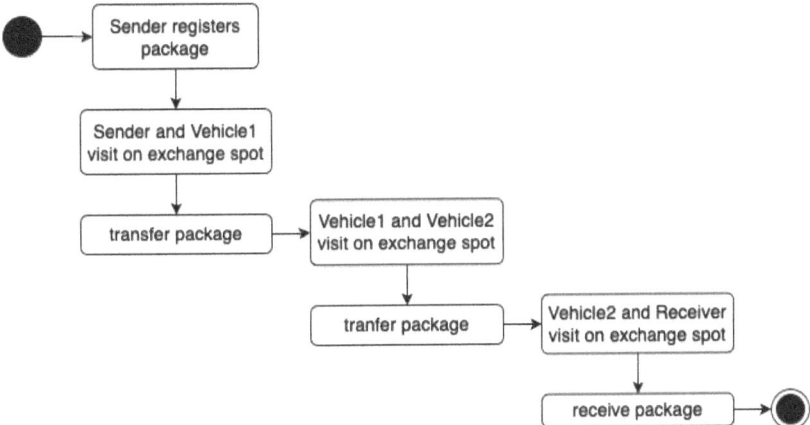

Fig. 2. Activity Diagram of a simple scenario.

tasked with picking up the parcel from the nearest exchange point. The vehicle then follows its route until it intersects with another vehicle's route, at which point the parcel is transferred at an exchange point. Person B is notified when the parcel is nearby, and the current vehicle meets the receiver at an exchange point to complete the delivery. This simplified example, is detailed in the activity diagram in Fig. 2, illustrates one sender, one receiver, three PI nodes for parcel handover, and two vehicles in the supply chain. The paper focuses on this high-level concept.

3.4   Design

The following section outlines the approach to addressing the requirements of the proposed concept using a MAS. It details how vehicles and parcels are modeled as agents, the role of the CARLA simulator, and the integration of Gaia-X components for ensuring security.

To meet the requirements R1-R4, a MAS is proposed. In an MAS, autonomous agents make local decisions without central control, allowing dynamic route planning to optimize the supply chain [6]. Vehicles and parcels will be modeled as agents, while CARLA will visualize parcel handling points (R5). Gaia-X components will ensure security (R6) by verifying the identities of senders, receivers, and vehicles. The scenario involves complex coordination of routes and destinations for both vehicles and parcels. The MAS will enable dynamic route planning to efficiently manage these routes. CARLA simulation

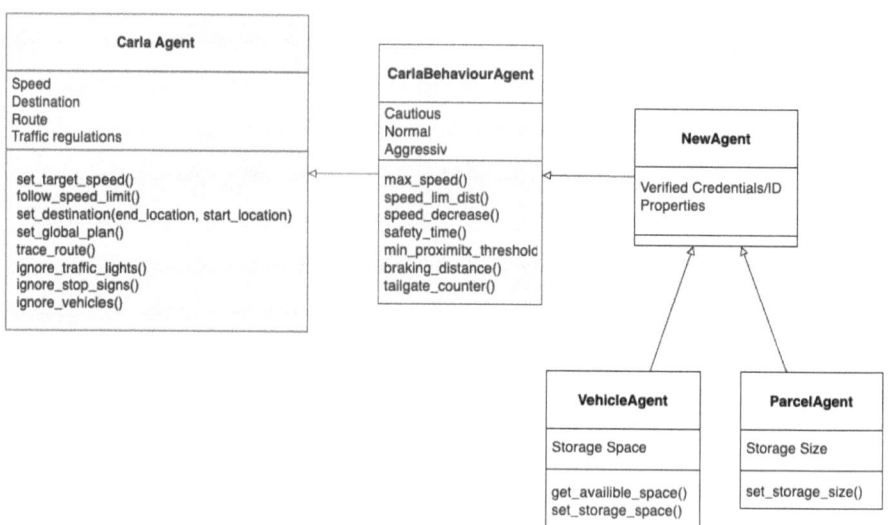

Fig. 3. Classdiagramm of Agents in CARLA Simulator and New Agents.

platform supports agent-based modeling. This paper introduces a new type of agent (Fig. 3), built upon CARLA's existing agent framework, which incorporates Gaia-X concepts and additional properties for secure data exchange. This agent features verified credentials for authentication and ensures trustworthiness within the PI.

The "NewAgent" class allows parcels to also function as agents, facilitating a dynamic fleet system where both vehicles and parcels interact autonomously. This integration of parcels as agents is crucial for effective route planning, considering parcel properties like size. The next step is to implement this idea based on the defined and analyzed requirements.

3.5   Implementation of the Proposed Concept

The proposed concept outlines an expandable DT design using the CARLA simulator to simulate parcel delivery between a sender and a receiver via a vehicle. This design incorporates Gaia-X Framework concepts and interfaces with the real world.

The implementation begins by initializing the CARLA simulation, ensuring the engine is operational with the default map, TOWN 10 [27]. The MQTT message protocol [28] is employed for communication. The workflow starts when the Cloud Parcel Service listens for MQTT topics, particularly "registerParcel". This service, detailed in this paper, operates in the cloud to facilitate parcel delivery communication. The Vehicle Parcel Service, which operates within the vehicle, serves as the system interface. Users or senders register parcels through the Gaia-X user interface, specifying details such as properties, pick-up location, and destination. This information is sent to the Cloud Parcel Service via MQTT.

Upon receiving the parcel information, the Cloud Parcel Service initiates Gaia-X Framework authentication to ensure secure communication between all entities. Once authenticated, CARLA and the Vehicle Parcel Service receive credentials via Gaia-X and connect with the MQTT broker, establishing a secure network. The Cloud Parcel Service then forwards the parcel information to CARLA using the "newParcel" MQTT topic. CARLA, receiving this information via MQTT, spawns a vehicle, an agent in the MAS, at the designated start location and places a person and parcel at the pick-up point within the simulated environment. The person, acting as an actor, ensures the parcel is correctly positioned for the vehicle. The vehicle, operating autonomously as an agent, is envisioned to adapt to real-time traffic conditions and demand changes in future work. However, this capability has not yet been implemented in the current design, which focuses solely on demonstrating the feasibility of integrating Gaia-X framework components within the PI. For now, the vehicle autonomously drives to the pick-up location, where it communicates with the actor to load the parcel.

Data from the real world is incorporated, including a camera view of the parcel being loaded. The simulated Vehicle Parcel Service identifies the parcel using a QR code and confirms it via the MQTT "claimparcel" topic. Once loaded, the vehicle drives to the destination. Upon arrival, CARLA spawns a person at the destination to receive the parcel. The vehicle notifies CARLA of its arrival, and the real actor moves the parcel out of the camera view to simulate unloading. The Vehicle Parcel Service then sends an MQTT message via "parcelDelivered" topic, and CARLA completes the delivery by placing the parcel next to the recipient.

This implementation links MAS, PI, Gaia-X and DT components, demonstrating their integration in a simplified scenario with one sender, one vehicle, and one receiver. The use of Gaia-X components, MAS, and the CARLA simulation platform, along with real-world data, highlights the feasibility of parcel delivery within a simulated DT environment of a PI, representing an initial proof of concept.

4   Conclusion

The environmental and public health challenges associated with expanding transport networks underscore the need for innovative solutions, as discussed in this paper. By leveraging the PI alongside Gaia-X security components and a MAS, we contribute to addressing these issues through secure, dynamic, and optimized freight transport.

Using the V-model approach, we established and implemented a framework that integrates DT and MAS within the CARLA simulation environment. By introducing a new standard agent in CARLA, equipped with Gaia-X framework components, the PI supports secure exchanges at transport nodes, ensuring that both vehicles and parcels can authenticate themselves and function as autonomous agents. This facilitates the dynamic adaptation of the supply chain in real-time.

Future extensions of this implementation, such as incorporating additional vehicle and parcel agents, will enable further optimization of delivery routes, enhance real-time coordination, and contribute to the development of a MAS for smart city logistics. The creation of DT in this context will also support the generation of knowledge graphs, promoting data-driven decision-making for sustainable logistics networks.

References

1. Savchenko, L., Semeriahina, M., Shevchenko, I.: Modeling daily dynamics of speed and fuel consumption for urban delivery means. Electr. Sci. J. Intellectualization Logistics Supply Chain Manag. #1 2020. **9**, 31–43 (2021). https://doi.org/10.46783/smart-scm/2021-9-3
2. Tran-Dang, H., Krommenacker, N., Charpentier, P., Kim, D.-S.: Toward the internet of things for physical internet: Perspectives and challenges. IEEE Internet Things J. 1–1 (2020). https://doi.org/10.1109/JIOT.2020.2971736
3. Ballot, E.: The Physical Internet, pages 719–734. Springer International Publishing, Cham (2019)
4. GAIA-X European Association for Data and Cloud. Gaia-x architecture document (2022). Accessed: 2024-05-29

5. Minerva, R., Lee, G.M., Crespi, N.: Digital twin in the IoT context: a survey on technical features, scenarios, and architectural models. Proceedings of the IEEE, 108(10):1785–1824 (2020)
6. Marik, V., McFarlane, D.: Industrial adoption of agent-based technologies. IEEE Intell. Syst. **20**(1), 27–35 (2005)
7. Chargui, M.R.T., Bekrar, A., Trentesaux, D.: Proposal of a multi-agent model for the sustainable truck scheduling and containers grouping problem in a road-rail physical internet hub. Int. J. Prod. Res. **58**(18), 5477–5501 (2020)
8. Kaup, S., Ludwig, A., Franczyk, B.: Framework artifact for the road-based physical internet based on internet protocols. arXiv:2106.08286. (2021)
9. Windolph, J., Kaup, S., Wehlitz, R., Franczyk, B., Ludwig, A.: Adapting a generic smart service platform architecture to the road-based physical internet. In ICEIS **1**, 749–756 (2023)
10. Kuhn, T.: Digitaler Zwilling (2017)
11. Grieves, M.: Digital twin: manufacturing excellence through virtual factory replication (2015)
12. Steinmetz, C., Schroeder, G.N., Rodrigues, R.N., Rettberg, A., Pereira, C.E.: Key-components for digital twin modeling with granularity: use case car-as-a-service. IEEE Trans. Emerg. Top. Comput. **10**(1), 23–33 (2022)
13. Clemen, T., et al.: Multi-agent systems and digital twins for smarter cities. In: Proceedings of the 2021 ACM SIGSIM Conference on Principles of Advanced Discrete Simulation, pages 45–55 (2021)
14. Mariani, S., Picone, M., Ricci, A.: About digital twins, agents, and multiagent systems: a cross-fertilisation journey. In: International Conference on Autonomous Agents and Multiagent Systems, pages 114–129. Springer (2022)
15. Pretel, E., Moya, A., Navarro, E., López-Jaquero, V., González, P.: Analysing the synergies between multi-agent systems and digital twins: a systematic literature review. Information and Software Technology, page 107503 (2024)
16. Weiss, G.: editor. Multiagent Systems. MIT Press, 2nd edition (2016)
17. Silva, J.C.V., Bazzan, A.L.C., Bordini, R.H.: Agents in traffic and transportation: exploring autonomic and multiagent systems in distributed environments. Multi. Grid Syst. **14**(2), 163–182 (2018)
18. Team CARLA. Carla simulator documentation. http://docs.carla.org. Accessed: 2024-05-28
19. Azarafza, M., Nayyeri, M., Steinmetz, C., Staab, S., Rettberg, A.: Hybrid reasoning based on large language models for autonomous car driving. arXiv preprint arXiv:2402.13602 (2024)
20. Isoda, T., Miyoshi, T., Yamazaki, T.: Digital twin platform for road traffic using Carla simulator. In: 2023 IEEE 13th International Conference on Consumer Electronics-Berlin (ICCE-Berlin), pages 47–50. IEEE (2023)
21. Steinmetz, C., et al.: Digital twins modeling and simulation with node-red and Carla. IFAC-Papersmisc, 55(19):97–102 (2022)
22. Brunnbauer, A., Berducci, L., Priller, P., Nickovic, D., Grosu, R.: Scenario-based curriculum generation for multi-agent autonomous driving. arXiv preprint arXiv:2403.17805 (2024)
23. Tardieu, H.: Role of gaia-x in the European data space ecosystem. In: Designing Data Spaces: The Ecosystem Approach to Competitive Advantage, pages 41–59. Springer International Publishing Cham (2022)
24. Braud, A., Fromentoux, G., Radier, B., Le Grand, O.: The road to European digital sovereignty with Gaia-x and IDSA. IEEE Network **35**(2), 4–5 (2021)

25. Chargui, T., Bekrar, A., Reghioui, M., Trentesaux, D.: Proposal of a multi-agent model for the sustainable truck scheduling and containers grouping problem in a road-rail physical internet hub. Int. J. Prod. Res. **58**(18), 5477–5501 (2019)
26. Fowler, K.R., Silver, C.L.: Developing and managing embedded systems and products methods, techniques, tools, processes, and teamwork. Expert guide. Newnes, Waltham, MA (2015)
27. Carla simulator. Carla default map. Accessed: 2024-05-28
28. MQTT.org. MQTT - The Standard for IoT Messaging

Low-Cost Architecture to Generate the Autonomous UAVs Position Data for Lab's Indoor Experimentation

Lucas C. Rech[1], Victor H. Garrett[1], Iohana A. T. Cabral[1],
Alvaro R. Cantieri[2], and Marco A. Wehrmeister[1]([⊠])(iD)

[1] Federal University of Technology - Paraná (UTFPR) Graduate Program in
Electrical and Computer Engineering (CPGEI), Curitiba, Brazil
{lucasrech,victorgarrett,iohana}@alunos.utfpr.edu.br,
wehrmeister@utfpr.edu.br
[2] Federal Institute of Technology - Paraná (IFPR) Applied Robotics and
Computation Laboratory (LaRCA), Pinhais, Brazil
alvaro.cantieri@ifpr.edu.br

Abstract. This work describes a low-cost and low-hardware-demanding architecture for generating position data for autonomous UAVs in indoor experiments. The approach is based on extracting data from a printed Augmented Reality tag fixed on the top of the Unmanned Aerial Vehicle (UAV) frame. This paper evaluates the reliability of the proposed architecture to provide valid position data for UAVs flying indoors. Such data is then processed by a PID position control algorithm running on a base station. Such a controller commands the displacement of a small multirotor UAV. The experimental results show an absolute position error less than 20.0 cm. The real-world experiments confirm the PID control's capability to maintain the UAVs flying correctly indoors along with a pre-programmed route. Compared with similar approaches found in the literature, the proposed architecture obtained similar performance; however, we employed less expensive hardware and reduced effort to expand the system to cover larger physical areas.

Keywords: Autonomous Unmanned Aerial Vehicle · indoor positioning system · AR-tag-based positioning system · low-cost systems

1 Introduction

Autonomous Unmanned Aerial Vehicles (autonomous UAVs) offer operational advantages for facing technical challenges in several areas, such as precision agriculture, large area mapping, cargo transport, search and rescue and surveillance, and others [19]. Among the different types of UAV, multirotor UAVs (also known as *"drones"*) have intrinsic characteristics (e.g. vertical take-off and landing, ability to land the rover in a static position during flight, high maneuverability, capacity to carry different types of sensors) that are sought for many kinds of real-world applications and scenarios.

© IFIP International Federation for Information Processing 2026
Published by Springer Nature Switzerland AG 2026
M. A. Wehrmeister et al. (Eds.): IESS 2024, IFIP AICT 760, pp. 99–112, 2026.
https://doi.org/10.1007/978-3-032-07102-6_9

Among technical challenges, precision positioning is a critical issue for performing drone experiments. The development of applications using this type of aircraft starts within a controlled environment in the lab, using small UAVs due to the reduced flight space. As the carrying capacity of such UAVs is usually limited, it is sometimes challenging to add sensors and processing hardware onboard the UAV; thus, auxiliary off-board systems for sensing and control are often employed. Some commercial systems provide this type of solution, such as *Vicon* tools [23]. However, the associated costs are sometimes very high and often not affordable for companies and universities in low-income countries.

Computer vision-based systems are commonly used to create indoor UAV positioning systems. However, such systems present some remarkable challenges: (i) detecting the moving target object within the captured images and identifying its position and orientation; and (b) image processing algorithms demand enormous amounts of resources, e.g. processing, memory, and energy. To address these issues, some work propose algorithms that process the captured image of small printed tags fixed to the vehicle, reducing the computational cost and improving the reliability of positioning readings.

This work proposes a simple and low-cost architecture to provide precision positioning to UAVs within the laboratory environment, allowing the implementation of experiments with small UAVs in autonomous flight indoors. The architecture uses a camera mounted on the roof of the flight area to capture images of small tags attached to each UAV and a computer to process the detection of objects and the identification of their poses. The system outputs 6-DoF position data of the target objects, allowing autonomous control of not only UAVs, but also ground robots. The architecture is intended to be implemented using ordinary low-cost hardware components such as a Webcam, small commercial aircraft, and a desktop or laptop personal computer. The results obtained show the feasibility of the proposed architecture. Even though the proposed architecture employed low-cost and less capable hardware components, the proposed solution achieves good results (i.e., it obtained an improved absolute error in the UAV's pose identification) compared to other related works. Such results are encouraging. They may allow experimental state-of-the-art research in aerial and multi-robot systems projects being carried out with a reduced equipment cost.

The remainder of this text is organized as follows. Section 2 reviews some related work. Section 3 presents the proposed architecture. Section 4 describes the experiments carried out to validate our proposal, while Section 5 discusses the results obtained. Finally, Section 6 draws final remarks and indicates future work directions.

2   Related Works

Precision positioning for UAVs in an indoor environment is based on techniques that capture the aircraft's coordinates using sensors positioned within the flight area or embedded in the aircraft. Most techniques are based on measuring the reception time of ultrasound signals, Ultra WideBand (UWB) positioning, and vision-based positioning with regular and depth cameras. Each technique has pros and cons related to the accuracy, robustness, coverage area, noise and signals interference immunity, hardware complexity, and deployment costs [21].

Ultrasound time-of-return techniques have low implementation complexity. The electronic circuits necessary for the emission and reception of the signals and measurements of the propagation time are simple. The works based on this technique are presented in [10, 16, 17]. The main weakness of the technique is to treat multiple reflections of signals in the environment and also when multiple sensors are employed [2].

Another common technique for developing precision positioning in an indoor environment is equipment based on the propagation of Ultra WideBand signals in a frequency range above 1.0GHz. This technique also presents limitations such as the treatment of multiple signal reflections, interference of signals transmitted by other equipment in the same frequency band, difficulty in embedding the processing hardware in the UAV, and limited coverage area, requiring equipment installation along the area to be covered. Some published works based on this technique are [13, 18, 22, 25] and a technical comparison between commercial tools is presented in the work [7].

Developing computer vision-based positioning systems with regular or depth cameras is a technique that does not require the use of additional hardware or specific circuits onboard the aircraft. The cost reduction of cameras and computers in the last decade allowed the development of systems with good results. Commercial vision-based positioning systems are available on the global market and have an accuracy of less than 1.0 cm. This type of product is an interesting way to create an experimental environment for UAV applications in indoor environments. However, the financial cost associated with such equipment is high, and it can be an impediment, especially in low-income countries where companies and universities can hardly afford the equipment acquisition cost. Such an issue justifies the development of alternative solutions. Thus, developing low-cost architectures that offer similar performance (such as the one proposed in this work) is an excellent approach to allow the development of autonomous UAV experiments within projects with low budgets.

A visual positioning system based on stereo images collected by two RGB cameras is presented [12]. The algorithm is written in C++ and OpenCV library. Two video cameras with 640x320 pixels frame resolution are aligned on the ground, pointing upside down at a small distance from each other. The algorithm calculates the stereo points on a laptop with an Intel i5 2.5Ghz processor and 4.0GB RAM, producing an output at 14 Hz. The system obtains a position error of 100.0 cm for the X, Y, and Z coordinates, as described by the authors. Another approach uses an arrangement of eight SCZE130M-GEHD cameras of 1280×720 pixels, with an infrared filter to capture images of a set of marker spheres fixed on a drone and calculate their position [5]. Image processing is performed on a Zynq-7000 SoC, dual-core ARM Cortex-A9 processor with an FPGA hardware acceleration. According to the authors, the results show a total error in (X, Y, and Z) about 10.0 cm in the flight experiments conducted.

Positioning architectures based on visual processing present high-performance hardware demands. A possible approach to minimize this demand is to use visual labels printed on paper, e.g., augmented reality tags [6,8,9]. Those tags have been developed to provide improved visual information and minimize the processing cost required for position calculations. A positioning algorithm based on the capture of images of a circular tag fixed to the ground is presented in [6]. The system runs on a single-core Intel Pentium M 1.86 GHz, with a processing time per round of 16 ms and a positioning error of less than 20.0cm for a height of 2.0 m. An arrangement with several tags pasted on walls around the flight area is presented in [9]. Images of these tags are captured by the front camera of a Bebop drone and processed off-board. The system is based on the AprilTag [11] tool. Experiments using a Vicon positioning system as ground truth show a positioning error of 0.6 m in the worst-case evaluation.

This work proposes using printed tags fixed on top of a small UAV whose images are captured by a Webcam placed in the ceiling of the flight area. A computer processes the tag detection algorithm and provides the 3D position and orientation of the tag used as the UAV pose. As demonstrated by our experiments, this architecture presents reduced hardware demands for its implementation, adequate performance, low cost, and scales for larger physical areas. Such an architecture allows working groups to run experiments with small multi-rotor UAVs in a laboratory with a low budget. We performed a literature survey that did not identify a similar approach and its evaluation in both simulated and real-world scenarios. To the best of our knowledge, no other similar approach uses commercial off-the-shelf (COTS) hardware with multirotor UAVs in lab experiments that require precise indoor positioning.

3   System Architecture and Its Components

A precise positioning architecture is proposed based on the image that captures small labels printed on paper and fixed on top of the aircraft to serve as a visual reference for the three-dimensional position processing.

The AR-Track Alvar Augmented Reality SDK, developed by the Finnish VTT Technical Research Centre [24], implements the visual position reference system. The AR Track Alvar [14] package provides ROS compatibility for this tool. AR-Tag images are recorded by the top-side camera and processed by this package that publishes position and orientation data on *ar_pose_marker* ROS Node. This tool provides flexible usage and excellent computational performance.

An ordinary computer works as a base station. This work uses a laptop with an Intel Core i7 processor, 16 GB RAM, and an Intel HD Graphics 520 (Skylake GT2) board. The laptop works with Ubuntu 16.4 LTS and ROS Kinect. A Logitec 720p webcam mounted on the roof of the flight area is connected to the base station using a USB cable. The AR-Tag package processes the tag image captured by the Webcam to calculate the position data. After processing, the package publishes position and orientation data on *ar_pose_marker* a ROS node. It is worth mentioning that any other system setup with similar features may achieve the results discussed in Sects. 4 and 5.

In addition, the base station runs the PID position control system, written in C++, and publishes velocity commands on specific ROS topics to displace the UAV, according to its programming interface. Tello drone is a commercial aircraft equipped has a flight stabilization embedded system, thus, the base station does not need to perform low-level stabilization and movement control. A mission control system uses a PID algorithm that implements control of vertical and horizontal positions during the UAV flight. The control algorithm is responsible for moving the aircraft in the experimentation arena according to the objective of the experiment. Figure 1 shows the logical diagram of the proposed architecture.

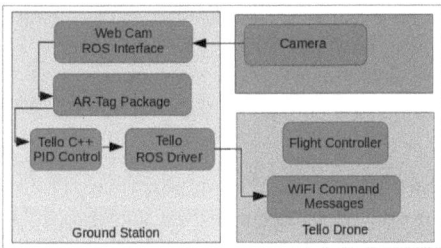

Fig. 1. Architecture block diagram   **Fig. 2.** Tello drone with Ar-Tag.

Laboratory experiments that employ one or more UAVs are generally described as a mission that includes a route and a set of actions that should be performed at each point. The route is a sequence of (x,y,z) coordinates plus the orientation at each point. To execute a route, the mission control sets a new target coordinate for the UAV once it reaches the previous coordinate by means of publishing messages into two ROS topics called */position* and */orientation*. The aircraft follows from the point where it is to the next point until reaching the position with a tolerance predetermined by the user, and after that, it publishes information about the position reached in a ROS topic called */position-achieved*. At the end of the proposed route, the system publishes a landing message through the */land* topic, or the aircraft is kept hovering until a new route is published.

To validate the proposed architecture, real-world experiments use a small-size DJI Tello drone that can receive commands from a computer through a 2.4 GHz 802.11n Wi-Fi connection. This aircraft's reduced size allows secure flight in constrained indoor spaces. A *tello_ driver* ROS package implements the communication the Tello drone and the ground station. A 6.0x6.0cm tag is fixed on the top of the aircraft. This size is defined to fit the aircraft frame, allowing the camera's visibility without interfering with flight stabilization. Figure 2 shows an image of the drone with the printed tag fixed on the frame.

4   Evaluation and Results

We have performed some experiments to evaluate the accuracy of the positioning data acquired through the proposed architecture and the performance of the control systems running on the base station using the data collected by the camera. As usual in many robotics research projects, we performed the initial experiments using a robotics simulator. The modeled scenarios run in a simulated environment created in both Coppelia Sim [4] and Gazebo [15] simulators; the goal is to evaluate the UAV absolute position error and its autonomous control using the AR-tag to provide the position data to the control algorithm. Thereafter real-world experiments have been executed in the laboratory environment; the goal is to evaluate the UAV control performance. A set of regular fluorescent lamps provides ordinary illumination for the room and they do not create any special conditions for the computer vision system. It is worth mentioning that illumination issues still negatively impact state-of-the-art computer vision systems [3,20].

4.1   Experiment 1: Simulating the Proposed Architecture with One UAV and One Camera

This initial experiment uses the Copellia Sim [4] simulation software. The goal is to analyze the feasibility of the proposed architecture. The simulated UAV runs a stabilization PID control implemented as LUA scripts, enabling the UAV to hover at a given position. Such a stabilization control implementation works similarly to the flight controller hardware and software of the Tello drones. A visual sensor working as an RGB camera with 512x512 pixel resolution and 50 degrees aperture angle (which are features found in a low-cost webcam) captures the tags fixed in the aircraft frame, and the AR-Tag Alvar package calculates the tag's position and publishes this information in */visualization_marker* ROS topic.

A ROS node implemented using the C++ client API receives this information and calculates the position of the nearest tag visualized by the camera. The node performs a reference transformation and publishes the results in */position* and */orientation* ROS topics. Another ROS node implements the mission control system that publishes a group of way-points on a */mission* topic, one at a time, to provide the next position and orientation points. Then, the LUA script that implements PID control for the UAV position takes this position data and performs the velocity calculations to displace the UAV to the next setpoint in space. The aircraft is programmed to fly inside the cameras' visible volume. The experiment runs with a hexacopter drone model with a 30.0cm radius with a 10.0x10.0cm tag placed on its top. The absolute position and the tag's calculated position data are captured during the UAV displacements.

Figure 3 shows the absolute position measurements of both AR-Tag and UAV compared to the planned route. Figure 3(a) shows (x,y) positions during a flight round while (b) shows the Z position. The Z measurements of the UAV position present an offset due to the position of the tag on the frame once the software uses the geometric center of the frame to set the absolute position of the UAV related to the simulation world coordinates. The absolute measurement error of all simulations was stored, and the mean and standard variation calculation results in 5.30 ± 2.75cm for the X coordinate, 4.78 ± 3.22cm for the Y coordinate, and 7.23 ± 4.21cm for the Z coordinate.

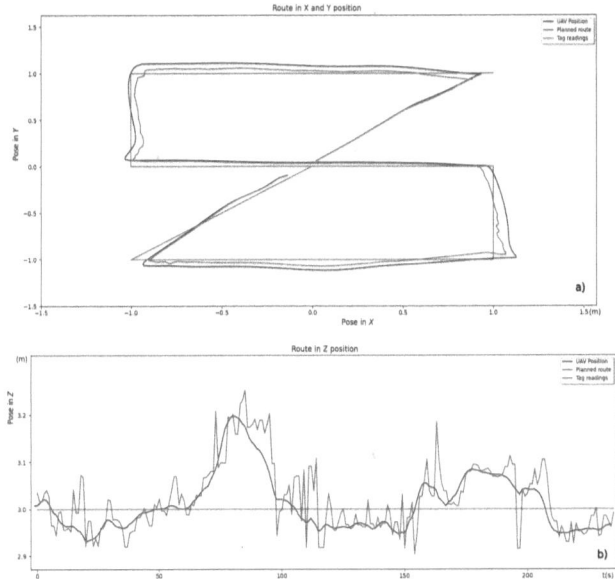

Fig. 3. Absolute position error for X, Y and Z coordinates in a 2D plot view.

4.2 Experiment 2: Evaluating the Absolute Position Measurements Using a Printed AR-Tag and Webcam in the Lab Environment

This experiment was performed using a real-world webcam and the printed AR-Tag inside the controlled environment of our lab. The goal is to evaluate the performance of the proposed architecture in a simple real-world scenario.

The UAV must keep its flight position within this area during all operations to allow its control. Two parameters must be considered to set the camera view volume[1]: a) the camera captures perspective volume; b) the limit of the tag capture and correct processing depending on the size of the tag. For this experiment, we employed a Logitec Webcam whose aperture is 60 degrees. Horizontal and vertical limits were set to the aircraft flight to ensure the camera keeps the visual link with the AR-tag. This limit defines a cubic flight volume for the route definition. Although this volume is small for some practical applications, adding more cameras in an array arrangement increases the size of this volume, as discussed in Sect. 4.4.

A 6.0x6.0 cm tag was manually displaced inside the field view of the camera in different positions including distinct heights and horizontal inclinations. The (x,y,z) position and yaw orientation data captured by the AR-Tag Alvar package were stored and pos-processed to calculate the absolute error mean and standard deviation. Table 1 presents the evaluation of the absolute position measurement of the tags captured inside the flight volume. This result shows that the proposed architecture provides accurate data to work on the UAV PID control algorithm. The absolute error is less than 3.90cm for the X-coordinate, 2.91cm for the

---

[1] the UAV must fly inside this volume (i.e., 3D area) to keep the visual reference provided by the tag thus enabling its control.

Y-coordinate, 5.94cm for the Z-coordinate, and 5.61 degrees for the Yaw orientation, considering a 95% confidence interval for the measurements. One may understand that position errors of such magnitude may impact negatively on the PID controllers, which is an issue when very high precision is demanded by the application. However, the experiment described in the next section shows that real-world UAV control works with acceptable performance besides this error magnitude, opening room for developing solutions for applications that demand good precision but can tolerate some imprecision in the UAV positioning. It is important to highlight that there is always a cost/performance trade-off. The proposed architecture is intended to be low-cost and affordable in opposite to expensive solutions which in turn are more accurate.

Table 1. X, Y, Z, and yaw measurements of the AR-Tag

Coordinates	Absolute Error (cm)							
[X,Y,Z,Yaw] (cm)	X mean	X SD	Y mean	Y SD	Z mean	Z SD	Yaw mean	Yaw SD
0;0;230;0	1.51	0.43	1.32	0.51	3.79	0.51	2.45	0.72
60;-35;230;0	2.33	0.33	1.69	0.40	4.27	0.55	3.12	0.95
35;60;230;0	2.62	0.51	1.41	0.49	4.35	0.63	3.10	1.08
-35;60;230;0	3.10	0.48	1.78	0.54	5.12	0.59	2.88	1.21
60;35;230;0	3.95	0.49	1.35	0.66	4.23	0.67	2.75	1.13
95% confidence Interval	2.70 ± 1.20		1.51 ± 1.40		4.35 ± 1.59		2.86 ± 2.75	

4.3   Experiment 3: Autonomous Flight of Tello Drone Using AR-Tag Position Readings

The goal is to evaluate whether it is possible to control the displacement of a real-world UAV within a controlled laboratory environment. This experiment involves flying a route that draws a square in 2D using one Tello drone. The Tello repeats the square flight three times at a fixed altitude of 1.5 m from the laboratory ground (2.0 m from the camera). The UAV starts at (0.0, 0.0) point and is commanded to displace to points [(0.5, 0.5); (-0.5, 0.5); (-0.5, 0.0); (0.5, 0.0); (0.5, 0.5)] returning to (0.0, 0.0) at the end of a round flight. A 5.0 cm tolerance indicates that the set point is achieved. A video showing the experiment round is available at https://youtu.be/uvLizXQkmjA. This video shows the complete route and status changes of the control algorithm in the left-side terminal window. The first number indicates the flight status for each set point, and the second indicates if the set point was achieved (0 - not achieved; 1 - achieved). The second terminal window shows the AR-Tag Alvar node publishing 6-DOF data. The PID algorithm calculations use only the AR-Tag Alvar position readings to work.

The results show that the proposed architecture enables the execution of the flights correctly, indicating its feasibility. The laboratory where the experiments are run lacks a ground truth positioning system to provide an absolute position error measurement. Hence, a manual measurement evaluates the aircraft position error in the endpoints of the square route by calculating the absolute distance of the aircraft frame origin to the (0,0,0)-point of camera frame and comparing it with the coordinates of the flight set point when the aircraft achieve the position (see Fig. 4). Table 2 shows the mean absolute error and standard deviation for the measured points of all experiment rounds.

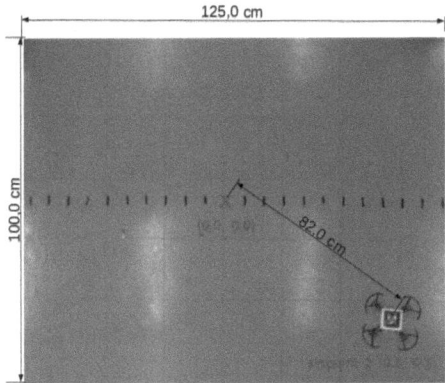

Fig. 4. Manual position error measurement example.

Table 2. Manual error measurements for ten flight rounds

Set Point	Abs Error Mean	SD
(0.0, 0.0)	4.70	5.78
(0.5, 0.5)	5.85	6.21
(-0.5, 0.5)	6.22	4.29
(-0.5, 0.0)	5.65	4.96
(0.5, 0.0)	4.91	3.80
(0.5, 0.5)	4.49	6.32

4.4 Experiment 4: Evaluating the Increase in the Covered Flight Area

The goal is to assess whether adding other cameras to the system increases the flight volume and the covered physical area. This experiment was carried out on the Gazebo simulator [15] and uses the Multi-robot Systems (MRS) [1] software stack to provide low-level control of the UAVs. The simulated scenario comprises four cameras arranged as a 5x5 meter square covering $25m^2$ ground area. We employed two UAVs to assess how the proposed architecture behaves when the pose of multiple UAVs should be detected, allowing the executing of experiments with cooperative multi-UAV systems.

Figure 5 gives an overview of the main components of this scenario. One can see the four cameras and two UAVs (blue boxes), and some ROS nodes (light orange boxes) that run on the ground station. The cameras have a resolution of 512x512 pixels (similar to experiment 01) and are placed 5 m above the ground.

Each camera is connected to an ROS node that processes the input image and publishes the 3D position of the UAVs on the ROS topic *UAV Sightings*. Each AR-Tag carries the ID information that is associated with a UAV. Multiple cameras can "see" the same UAV; thus, multiple observations of the same UAV at distinct relative positions (related to a given individual camera) are published. Then, the *Tag Management* node processes all messages representing the multiple observations within a given duration to calculate the absolute position of each UAV. Such an absolute position is then forwarded to the PID position control system to control each UAV displacement, as previously discussed.

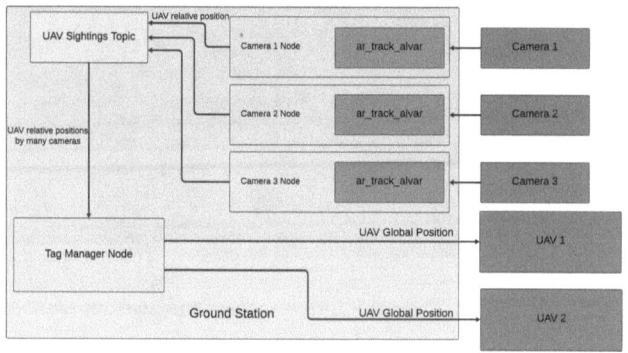

Fig. 5. Main components used in experiment 4.

Two UAVs flew three distinct routes: (a) a linear route flying back and forth (see Fig. 6); (b) a route that formed a triangle shape (see Fig. 6); and (c) a route that formed a square shape (see Fig. 6c). In all routes, the altitude was kept at 1.9 m during the whole trajectory, i.e., only the x and y coordinates changed from way-point to way-point. A video of the simulation of the route (c) with two UAVs can be seen at https://youtu.be/8cI_SJOGXPw

Figure 6 depicts the trajectory of the two UAVs. The X- and Y-axes depict the X- and Y-positions of each UAV. The absolute position provided by Gazebo is depicted as "UAV position" (and is considered the ground truth), and the absolute position processed by the proposed architecture, based on the AR-Tag, as "UAV measured". One can see that both UAVs performed the three trajectories

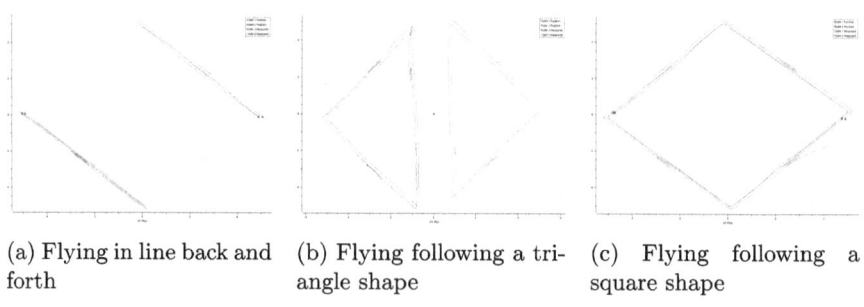

(a) Flying in line back and forth

(b) Flying following a triangle shape

(c) Flying following a square shape

Fig. 6. Absolute (x,y) position for two UAV

satisfactorily. Also, these charts show that the ground truth positions and the calculated ones are close.

Table 3 shows the mean and standard deviation of the absolute error for (x, y, z)-position of the two UAVs. One can see that the mean error for both X- and Y-coordinates varies between 13.47cm and 16.54cm whereas between 14.92cm and 15.29cm for the Z-coordinate. On the one hand, the average absolute position error is low and coherent with the results obtained in other experiments, i.e., expanded architecture presents similar performance. On the other hand, in this experiment, the covered physical area is considerably greater than in the previous experiments. These results are satisfactory for many sorts of UAV applications and show the feasibility of the proposed architecture to allow experimenting with multiple UAVs flying within larger physical areas at a lower and affordable cost.

Finally, it is worth mentioning that adding the three extra cameras (in comparison with experiments 01–03) imposes a neglectful effort since we only needed to instantiate new ROS nodes and connect them to the ROS topics of each individual camera. The *Tag Manager* node has been implemented to be scalable; thus, additional cameras can be easily added to the architecture. The only effort is to instantiate additional camera nodes that publish the position data of UAVs on the topic *UAV sightings*, which are later processed by the *Tag Manager* node.

Table 3. Absolute position error for two UAVs following distinct routes

Coordinates	Absolute Error (cm)					
	X avg.	X SD	Y avg.	Y SD	Z avg.	Z SD
Line	13.47	11.50	13.74	10.69	15.20	04.13
Triangle	16.54	10.41	14.06	11.70	15.48	04.57
Square	13.90	12.53	13.97	11.47	14.92	06.08

5   Discussion

This work's main goal is to investigate the feasibility of using the proposed architecture to build a low-cost and less hardware-demanding indoor position system to enable experiments for autonomous UAV systems in a laboratory environment. Analysis of the experimental results indicates that the architecture offers consistent position data and repeatability for the PID control algorithm in both simulation and real-world experiments.

Simulated experiments showed an absolute error mean of less than 15.0cm for the horizontal position and 20.0cm for the vertical position of the UAV for all the experiments, considering a 95% confidence interval for the measurements. This value is consistent with the AR-Tag measurement error shown in Fig. 3. The visual sensor used in the simulation is set to a 512x512 pixel resolution. Such a low resolution was chosen to provide an experimental condition similar to a real-world camera with noise and variations in the image capturing to evaluate the performance of the PID position algorithm. Higher resolution cameras provide better position data inputs, decreasing the UAV position error.

The results of the second experiment indicate that the tag capture and processing using the Webcam with regular laboratory illumination is adequate to generate position data for real-world experiments. These results were achieved with normal indoor conditions and low-cost hardware (Webcam); however, it is possible to achieve better results by improving the hardware quality. The absolute position error (Table 1) is lower than 8.60cm, which would be inadequate for experiments that demand very precise positioning. Still, such an error magnitude is satisfactory to evaluate the performance of the PID position algorithm.

Manual calculation of the position error in the UAV set-points presents consistent values compared with simulation and the static measurements executed in experiment 02. As mentioned, it is important to highlight that this absolute position error may be high for precise positioning indoor system applications. However, it is possible to increase this performance using a better quality camera, improved and controlled light conditions, and larger tags (if possible).

A comparison between the obtained results and the related works that use tags is shown in Table 4. The proposed architecture achieves better results in position error than two similar works and is also closer to the other two. Compared with the hardware demands, the proposed architecture presents less complexity than all the other works. Also, this architecture allows for an increase in the coverage area by adding more cameras, as demonstrated in experiment 04. This seems to be complex in the approaches proposed in the four related works.

Finally, as demonstrated by the flight experiments, the proposed architecture is able to keep the UAV in the desired route and within the flight area in all the experiments. Considering that the AR-Tag data is the only position information for the PID control algorithm work, using additional data and Sensor Fusion techniques could bring these results to higher confidence levels.

Table 4. Comparison between the proposed architecture and similar approaches

Work	Proposed architecture	[12]	[13]	[14]	[15]
Absolute Error	20.0 cm	100.0 cm	10.0 cm	20.0 cm	60.0 cm
Hardware complexity	Low	High	High	Low	Mediun

6   Conclusions and Future Works

The present work proposes a simple and low-cost architecture to provide 3D position data from autonomous UAVs while they are flying in an indoor environment. The experiments confirm the good performance and reliability of the proposed low-cost architecture, allowing the proper control of a small UAV using only the position data generated by the visual processing of the AR-Tag. Experiments using real-work UAVs and a webcam show a maximum error of 20cm in processing the absolute position of the UAV. This performance is adequate for many real-world applications that use multiple UAVs in indoor environments, e.g., stock inventory and infrastructure inspection.

The architecture is simple to build and expand and can be improved by using superior-performance hardware if one can afford it. The low cost and easy access to the necessary equipment to implement this solution are advantages of this architecture compared with other approaches found in the literature, offering a quick start to new research working in applications with small autonomous UAVs. The proposed architecture is flexible and allows changing the underlying execution platform easily, as demonstrated in the experiments. In the experiments, we used different simulators and real-world components such as a webcam and a Tello drone. The results indicate that the proposed architecture is an affordable solution enabling experiments for a considerable range of real-world applications in laboratory conditions.

Additional work is planned as future work to improve the proposed architecture as follows: (a) investigating and evaluating other camera models; (b) assessing the best trade-off between AR-tag size, UAV size, and its absolute position detection; and (c) performing additional real-world experiments to evaluate the effectiveness of increasing the flight area coverage by adding more low-cost webcams and (multiple) cheaper computing devices (e.g., Raspberry Pi) to run the implemented software system.

Acknowledgments. This study was funded by CAPES, grant 88887.974732/2024-00.

Disclosure of Interests. The authors have no competing interests to declare that are relevant to the content of this article.

References

1. Baca, T., et al.: The MRS UAV system: pushing the frontiers of reproducible research, real-world deployment, and education with autonomous unmanned aerial vehicles. J. Intell. Rob. Syst. **102**(1), 26 (2021)
2. Berger, G.S., et al.: Sensorial testbed for high-voltage tower inspection with UAVs. In: Tardioli, D., et al. (eds.) ROBOT2022: Fifth Iberian Robotics Conference, pp. 353–364. Springer International Publishing, Cham (2023)
3. Bhattacharya, S., Spooner, C., Wemlinger, E.: Vision guided drone flight for entering confined spaces for inspection. In: 2023 IEEE International Conference on Industrial Technology (ICIT), pp. 1–4 (2023)
4. Copellia Robotics: CoppeliaSim (2019). https://www.coppeliarobotics.com/
5. Deng, C., Wang, S., Huang, Z., Tan, Z., Liu, J.: Unmanned aerial vehicles for power line inspection: a cooperative way in platforms and communications. J. Commun. **9**(9), 687–692 (2014)
6. Eberli, D., Scaramuzza, D., Weiss, S., Siegwart, R.: Vision based position control for MAVs using one single circular landmark. J. Intell. Rob. Syst. **61**, 495–512 (2011)
7. Granja, F.S., Ruiz, A.R.J.: UWB location systemsâĂŕ: indoor performance analysis. IEEE Trans. Instrum. Meas. **66**(8), 1–12 (2017)

8. Jayatilleke, L., Zhang, N.: Landmark-based localization for unmanned aerial vehicles. SysCon 2013 - 7th Annual IEEE International Systems Conference, Proceedings, pp. 448–451 (2013)

9. Kayhani, N., et al.: Improved tag-based indoor localization of UAVs using extended Kalman Filter. Proceedings of the 36th International Symposium on Automation and Robotics in Construction, ISARC 2019 (Isarc), 624–631 (2019)

10. Khosiawan, Y., Nielsen, I.: A system of UAV application in indoor environment. Prod. Manuf. Res. **4**(1), 2–22 (2016)

11. Laboratory, A.R.: AprilTags Visual Fiducial System (2024). https://april.eecs.umich.edu/software/apriltag

12. Mustafah, Y.M., Azman, A.W., Akbar, F.: Indoor UAV positioning using stereo vision sensor. Proc. Eng. **41**(Iris), 575–579 (2012)

13. Nguyen, T.M., Zaini, A., Guo, K., Xie, L.: An ultra-wideband-based multi-UAV localization system in GPS-denied environments (10 2016)

14. Niekum, S.: ar_track_alvar Ros Package (2024). http://wiki.ros.org/ar_track_alvar

15. Open Robotics: Gazebo (2024). https://gazebosim.org

16. Paredes, J.A., et al.: 3D indoor positioning of UAVs with spread spectrum ultrasound and time-of-flight cameras. Sensors **18**(1) (2018). Article #89

17. Pérez, M., Gualda, D., Vicente, J., Villadangos, J., Ureña, J.: Review of UAV positioning in indoor environments and new proposal based on us measurements. In: CEUR Workshop Proc. vol. 2498, pp. 267–274 (2019)

18. Shule, W., et al.: Uwb-based localization for multi-uav systems and collaborative heterogeneous multi-robot systems. Procedia Computer Science **175**, 357–364 (2020), 17th Int. Conf. on Mobile Systems and Pervasive Computing (MobiSPC), 15th Int. Conf. on Future Networks and Communications (FNC), 10th Int. Conf. on Sustainable Energy Information Technology

19. Skorobogatov, G., Barrado, C., Salamí, E.: Multiple UAV systems: a survey. Unmanned Systems **08**(02), 149–169 (2020)

20. Sun, X., et al.: Transtracking for UAV: an autonomous real-time target tracking system for UAV via transformer tracking. In: 2021 International Conference on Intelligent Technology and Embedded Systems (ICITES), pp. 102–107 (2021)

21. Tariq, Z.B., Cheema, D.M., Kamran, M.Z., Naqvi, I.H.: Non-GPS positioning systems: a survey. ACM Comput. Surv. **50**(4) (2017)

22. Tiemann, J., Ramsey, A., Wietfeld, C.: Enhanced UAV indoor navigation through slam-augmented UWB localization. In: 2018 IEEE International Conference on Communications Workshops (ICC Workshops), pp. 1–6 (2018)

23. VICON: Vicon tracker (2024). https://www.vicon.com/software/tracker/

24. VTT Technical Research Centre of Finland: Augmented reality - 3d tracking (2017). http://virtual.vtt.fi/virtual/proj2/multimedia/

25. You, W., et al.: Data fusion of UWB and IMU based on unscented kalman filter for indoor localization of quadrotor UAV. IEEE Access **8**, 64971–64981 (2020)

Author Index

© IFIP International Federation for Information Processing 2026
Published by Springer Nature Switzerland AG 2026
M. A. Wehrmeister et al. (Eds.): IESS 2024, IFIP AICT 760, p. 113, 2026.
https://doi.org/10.1007/978-3-032-07102-6

MIX

Papier | Fördert
gute Waldnutzung

FSC® C083411

Zeitfracht Medien GmbH
Ferdinand-Jühlke-Straße 7
99095 Erfurt, Deutschland
produktsicherheit@kolibri360.de